Contents

The Border Patrol Ate My Dust

Alicia Alarcón

English translation by
Ethriam Cash Brammer de Gonzales

Arte Público Press
Houston, Texas

To all the men and women who shared their stories with me.

This volume is made possible through the City of Houston through The Cultural Arts Council of Houston, Harris County.

Recovering the past, creating the future

Arte Público Press
University of Houston
452 Cullen Performance Hall
Houston, Texas 77204-2004

Cover design by Giovanni Mora.
Cover art by Noé Hernández, "The New American Cowboy."

Alarcón, Alicia 1953–
Migra me hizo los mandados, La. English
The Border Patrol Ate My Dust / [compiled by] Alicia Alarcón ; English translation by Ethriam Cash Brammer.
p. cm.
Originally published as: La migra me hizo los mandados. Houston, TX: Arte Publico, 2002.
ISBN 1-55885-432-0 (pbk. : alk. paper)
1. Central American Americans—California—Biography. 2. South American Americans—California—Biography. 3. Immigrants—California—Biography. 4. California—Biography. 5. Central American Americans—California—Social conditions. 6. South American Americans—California—Social conditions. 7. Immigrants—California—Social conditions. 8. Central America—Emigration and immigration—Case studies. 9. South America—Emigration and immigration—Case studies. 10. United States—Emigration and immigration—Case studies. I. Alarcon, Alicia, 1953– II. Brammer, Ethriam Cash. III. Title.
F870.C34M54 2004
979.4'00468728—dc22 2004048530
CIP

∞ The paper used in this publication meets the requirements of the American National Standard for Information Sciences—Permanence of Paper for Printed Library Materials, ANSI Z39.48-1984.

4 5 6 7 8 9 0 1 2 3 10 9 8 7 6 5 4 3 2 1

Dark Angel

The day that my father came home with the news that they had closed the factory was the same day that President José López Portillo proclaimed the beginning of a new era of prosperity for Mexico and all of its people. The president said, "Every Mexican citizen must know that 1979 is a year of economic prosperity. No one need doubt that Mexico is on its way toward progress and that our nation has vanquished the dark forces which had hoped to tie it down to the past." He also stated, "Mexico is the only country in the world in which three super giant petroleum deposits have been discovered, in this decade alone."

One week earlier, the San Luis Potosí newspapers had published articles about the surge in petroleum production in Chicontepec, Veracruz; Sabinas, Coahuila; and the Gulf of Mexico. During his speech, the president promised, "The petroleum bonanza will reach every corner of the Mexican republic."

"Do you believe anything that the president is saying?" asked my father.

I was seventeen years old, and I believed everything that I heard, except for what the president had to say. I had heard my mother say time and time again, "Promises, promises . . . they never do anything." And so I replied, "No, Pop. Promises, promises . . . they never do anything."

He smiled. Then he got up from the wooden table and turned off the television. I kept staring at the screen until all of the little white dots had disappeared, along with the president's face. He returned to his seat, looking out of the corner of his eye at my mother, who was pouring beans out onto sizzling lard.

"So are we going to go up North, or what?"

The sizzling of the lard prevented me from hearing the question clearly. My eyes followed the smoke that rose up from the frying pan and shattered against the rafters of the ceiling. My five brothers and sisters were playing in the other room. The room that my parents and I were in was called "the big room." We called it that because that was where we had all of our furniture: the table with the four chairs, the icebox where we stored the milk, the stove, and a black-and-white television set that my father had very proudly placed next to the window six months earlier. "Now we don't have to go over to the neighbors' to watch TV."

My father continued, "I have a friend who told me that it was easy to sneak across the border. Since you're the oldest, it's your responsibility to accompany me."

I was about to ask him which city in the United States we were going to go to, when the conversation was suddenly interrupted. My mother's face was covered in tears as she stood before us. She had been listening to us.

"Why don't you look for a job around here? Martín's too young to go off gallivanting around with you."

The plan to cross the border had been momentarily cancelled. Months went by, and the bonanza that the president promised all of Mexico had not reached a single corner of San Luis Potosí. Mexico may have had large petroleum deposits, but my father still had no job. "We don't have anything for you right now," they would tell him. "Try back again some other time."

I had to drop out of school when there was no more money to buy books. I started to go look for work with my father. Jobs were scarce and poorly paid, but we managed to put aside a little bit of money to travel north.

The idea of going to the United States seemed more and more attractive to me with each passing day. I got even more excited when my father told me that we would be going to Los Angeles. I knew that Hollywood was in Los Angeles, and I thought that I might be able to meet some of the stars that came out on television.

We ate dinner in silence. The television was on. Jorge Díaz Serrano, the director of PEMEX (Petróleos Mexicanos), was being interviewed on account of the inauguration of the new refinery in Salina Cruz, Oaxaca, on the Pacific Coast. "With this new refinery, we will now be able to produce 1,335,000 barrels per day, as opposed to only 965,000 barrels a day previously. Currently, Mexico exports 900,000 barrels of petroleum daily, which is determined to have an equivalent exportation value of approximately $19,200,000. The price of Mexican crude is currently set at $32 a barrel, making it the third most expensive in the world, following behind Libya at $34.72 and Nigeria at $34.48 . . . . Mexico is experiencing prosperity . . ."

Once again, the white dots on the television and the face of Díaz Serrano disappeared, just like the president's face had disappeared months earlier, and just like everything else on that screen would disappear whenever my father would say, "That's enough TV," and turn it off. That was his way of getting our attention.

"Martín, call your brothers and sisters."

We all sat down to listen to him. My mother had her back turned to us, she was facing the stove. We didn't have to see her face to know that she was crying.

"Martín is going with me because he's the oldest. We're

going to cross the border by train. Look after your mother while we're away. Be good. And, God willing, we'll see each other again very soon."

Upon hearing this, my mother's shoulders began to shake almost convulsively. My father came up to her from behind. He whispered something into her ear. She turned around quickly and threw her arms around his neck. She started to sob into his chest. She begged for him to stay. The scene enveloped us in silence. Upon seeing my mother cry, my brothers and sisters began to do the same.

My father, alarmed by all of my brothers' and sisters' tears, tried to make everyone laugh. "Well, wouldn't you know? This red chile sauce that Mom made is making us all cry."

At that moment, I felt a sharp pain between my ribs. Everyone in my family was crying except for me. Suddenly, a kind of sadness that I had never felt before came over me. I might never see my brothers and sisters, my mother, my friends, or even the city that I grew up in ever again. The pain became more intense. It was as if my heart had detached itself from my chest and passed through my ribs, opening each one of them to make way for it to cross through. For a long time, it was difficult for me to breathe.

We left just before dawn. My mother made every effort to appear calm. She handed us a big bundle filled with bologna sandwiches, and she filled up a bottle with water for us to drink on the road. I wanted to hug her and keep holding onto her like I did when I was a little boy. But those days were gone. Now it was my duty, as the oldest son in the family, to go with my father. I asked my mother for her blessing, and I kissed her hand as I left. I never looked back.

The bus station was not far from where we lived. After purchasing two tickets to Mexicali, the money we had was drastically reduced, leaving little left for our trip. The sandwiches my mother made, a bottle of water, and her blessings were all that we took with us from our beloved, but "God-forsaken" San Luis Potosí. We sat down to await the bus' departure.

A newspaper that someone had discarded provided us with the latest news. I opened it. The article covered almost the entire page.

> JORGE DÍAZ SERRANO ACCUSED OF ILLICIT DEALINGS
>
> The leader of the workers' opposition party, Heberto Castillo, brought charges against the Director of PEMEX (Petróleos Mexicanos) directly to the president, José López Portillo, accusing the director of taking advantage of his position for his own personal benefit and increasing his own wealth . . .

We reached Mexicali after two days and two nights. When we got off the bus, it was like stepping into a furnace. Our legs were sore and it was difficult to walk. It was May 1980, and they told us that summer was only just beginning there. We had no water and no money. All that my father knew was that we were going to jump the border, but he didn't know exactly how; he didn't know which train was leaving for Los Angeles, either. Asking around, they showed us how to get to the train station. We walked slowly. We didn't have enough money to take another bus. My "milk bottle" boots—that's what they were called in San Luis Potosí—were so tight on my feet that it seemed like they had suddenly grown. I was able to hide the pain by walking upright. It comforted me to think that we would soon reach the train and from there, we'd go to Los Angeles. How could I have imagined the adventures that were still in store for us?

We arrived at the train station. In order not to arouse any suspicions, we pretended to be passengers who were simply taking a trip. We were surveying the place when two individuals approached us. One was called "The Angel"; he was actually from Mexico City. The other was from Michoacan. We were a little distrustful of them at first, but after a while, and because we didn't know what to do or where to go, we told them that we wanted to get across to the other side. The two men had the same filthy and haggardly appearance that we did, perhaps even worse. The Angel gave the distinct impression that he was an adventurer and that he knew everything about everything. He gave us the lowdown on what we had to do and how to do it. He took us to the train. We left through the main lobby, circling around the building until we were hidden back behind it, far from the main entrance, yet very close to a number of railroad cars. The Angel pointed us to a few rotary gondolas, the ones used for transporting coal, the kind with the open hoppers.

"That's where we're going," he told us.

"But, they'll see us," we said naively. "How are we supposed to keep ourselves covered?"

Impatiently, The Angel replied, staring at us the way one looks at a pair of numbskulls, "You really are a couple of dummies, aren't you? You're not going up top, you're going down on the bottom, in a little iron sill, between the gondola and the wheels of the train."

I couldn't understand how we were going to fit down there, especially since I could see from there just how narrow the space really was.

He warned us: "Only about half an ass is going to fit inside. So, you'll have to hold on tight."

According to The Angel's instructions, we needed to hide ourselves beneath the coal cars before the inspections began. So that's what we did. We stayed there until seven o'clock in the evening. The Angel assured us that the train was going to leave around eight.

It was an acute angle of iron, a tiny draft sill that we could barely squeeze into. We were in a kind of squatting, ducking position. It was the only place where the inspectors on this and the other side of the border could not see us. And in that squatting position, we saw an enormous wheel in front of us. It looked gigantic. The terror I felt made it appear twice its normal size. Each one of us was positioned in an opposite corner of the same railcar. It was eight o'clock, and the train had yet to depart. We were still inside. Motionless. Hungry and sweating profusely due to the heat that baked the metal boxes that surrounded us. In a single hour, we had consumed half a gallon of the water The Angel brought with him. We calculated that it shouldn't take much longer. There we were, squatting, not speaking, just listening to each sound that came to us from the outside until ten o'clock at night. Suddenly, a thunderous noise jarred us. The roars of thunder were none other than other railcars being attached to the car that we were in. With each new addition, we felt as if we were going to be shot out like a canon, but we held on for all our worth. There were eight thunderclaps, eight colossal collisions, eight times that we thought we were going to be shot out from our sills and end up under the giant wheel. I don't know how we were able to withstand the jolting. The Angel shouted, "You better hang on tight if you want to make it out alive."

Then, there was a brief moment of silence, followed by a long whistle. We started to pray, thanking God for not allowing us to be crushed under the wheel. The Angel had estimated that we would reach the United States in about a day. Once again, his calculation was off.

The train advanced, sometimes fast, sometimes slow. It was as if the engineer was on his own time schedule. With my eyes closed, I could still recall the shriek of the sizzling lard making contact with the beans. I saw my mother in one of the corners of the big room. I remembered my sisters' conversations. Their memory helped me not to give in. I couldn't give in. How could I? There I was, in a crouched position, like a fly that hopes to cross undetected so it won't die squashed in one fatal blow. Hours went by. Fatigue began to put our lives in danger. Up until that moment, what had saved us had been the strength of our will and the strength in our muscles. Only by pressing against the sides of the space under the railcar with our hands and feet would we survive. If we let go, the wheel in front of us, with its guillotine blade, would cut us to pieces. We couldn't even blink. But blinking was inevitable.

We had already been traveling for a very long time; hunger, exhaustion and fatigue were beginning to weaken my muscles. I was just about to close my eyes when a shout woke me. It was like a miracle. It was my father's voice, "How're you feeling? Don't go to sleep on me now! Just hold on tight!"

My father's voice gave me the strength to hold on. I was terrified of falling asleep. I began to yell back to him. From that moment on, we talked to each other every now and again. I discovered that his voice was coming from a hole, which allowed me to hear him from the other side of the train. Whenever the train picked up speed, the sparks from the wheels flew into my face. The hours went by. I'm not sure how many. Then, suddenly, the train began to lose speed. "We must be getting to Los Angeles," I thought.

Quiet, motionless, I waited for The Angel's instructions. About two hours went by and nothing. I ventured to stretch one of my legs, then the other. There I was, alternating each leg, when suddenly I saw someone right in front of me. His eyes were sunken. He was dirty. Perhaps even dirtier than myself. I looked down at his pants. I wasn't the only one who had wet himself. It was The Angel. He told me not to get out because the train had only stopped there in order to detach a few freight cars. He told my father the same thing.

Then, like a ghost, The Angel disappeared into the night, returning to his place once again.

The claps of thunder were heard again, but this time they were accompanied by voices. It was the inspectors who checked the railcars. They carried lamps in their hands. Their footsteps got closer and closer to us. They shuffled their feet in the loose gravel. For a moment I stopped breathing. I was sure that they had spotted us. They said something in English. To my surprise, their voices went away along with their footsteps. I began to relax. I felt a warm, gentle liquid course down my legs. I was peeing on myself. I was still urinating when we experienced the worst pounding that I had ever felt. I was sure that by jerking around the railcars, they were hoping to see us spill out of the iron sills like vomit. I held on with even greater intensity. It was like hell on wheels. Not only were there horizontal jolts, but there were perpendicular ones as well; the pounding came from every direction. It seemed to last forever. My heart raced faster and faster. I felt so many different emotions all at the same time: hopelessness, powerlessness, and rage. I commended my soul to the Virgin of San Juan de los Lagos. I was sure that they were doing it on purpose because, from my hiding place, I could hear the voices, the shouts, and the laughter of those who were jostling the railcars.

My father began to shout: "Don't you even think about getting down! They haven't seen us yet! Just hold on tight!"

I don't know how long it took before that hell came to an end. We heard a huge bang. The noise was so loud, like something had crashed into our train. As with every good tragedy, there was calm after the storm. Without understanding what had taken place, I saw The Angel before me.

"They attached the engine to our car," he whispered to me. And then he disappeared as quickly as he had appeared.

Once again I felt the train pulling away, faster now than

before. The sparks became small fires extinguishing as soon as they made contact with the tracks. The water was gone. We had traveled for two days without eating. I concentrated on remembering the smell of cilantro over tender nopal cactus and the taste of jamaica water. "Drink it. It's good for you." The diced pork that we would buy at the butcher shop on the corner. The aroma of chiles and tomatoes steaming on top of the meat. The avocado and cheese tacos in the afternoon. Sleep taunted me. I thought about Hollywood. I imagined it filled with lights like a giant reflector above the asphalt, the stars signing autographs on the sidewalks.

The wheel in front of me helped to keep me awake; if I were to fall beneath it, I would surely die. There was a moment when I thought that I was dreaming, that none of those things were really happening to me. My father's voice brought me back to reality.

"Martín, we're almost there. Son, don't let go."

"Don't worry. I'm holding tight."

"Do you remember the first time that I took you to the movies?"

"Yes. Yes, I remember."

"Tell me, son. Tell me what the movie was about."

"I can't remember the movie."

"I can. It was about wrestling. It had El Santo in it."

For the rest of the trip, he told me about El Santo—Mexico's most famous wrestler—about San Luis Potosí, about the day that he met my mother, about how my grandfather tried to run him off. He wouldn't stop talking to me. My eyelids felt like they were made of lead. My hands began to give way, the guillotine just a few inches away. I could hear the sound of the wheels on the tracks getting closer and closer. I had reached the end of my rope.

Then, suddenly, the train came to a halt. The corpse-like figure of a man stood beneath me. It was dark. I wanted to wake up. I thought that it was Death himself. "Had I fallen beneath the guillotine?" It was The Angel. Two sunken eyes in two dark sockets.

His words, in an almost unintelligible whisper, were spoken quickly: "Get down. We're here."

"We're here? Angel, are you sure we made it?"

"Yes, this is San Bernardino."

It was the first time that I had ever heard the name of that particular saint.

"Are we close to Los Angeles?"

"No. Los Angeles is about an hour and a half from here. Get down," The Angel repeated.

I was so excited. I never would have guessed that cities in the United States would be named after angels and saints. I wanted to jump off, but my legs wouldn't let me. The Angel was losing his patience. I wanted to spring out, but my body wouldn't respond. The Angel approached me and helped me down. Slowly, I tried to stretch my legs; they trembled.

"This is San Bernardino," The Angel declared.

"Are you sure that we're in the United States?" I insisted.

"We're in the United States," he repeated.

My father came up to us, staggering. We helped the man from Michoacan to get down; it took him even longer than me to stretch his legs. The skin on his face clung to his skull.

The Angel gave us some more instructions. "Now, we walk. Make sure that nobody sees you."

We walked along the side of a road. Little by little, the feeling returned to our legs. We passed through some trees. At times, we would lose sight of The Angel, who cloaked himself in the darkness. We had to walk quickly to keep up with him. We kept stumbling. We followed the train tracks. We continued for an hour without stopping.

"We're going to go up to the freeway."

"Freeway" was a new word for me. We decided to follow it. A great, big highway opened up in front of us. It was lighted; we could see each other's faces. The man from Michoacan looked very tired, perhaps even more tired than we were. The sun was just beginning to rise. The Angel led us to a dirt road that ran parallel to the freeway. It was deserted. My boots grew heavy. I stopped for a moment to look at my blistered feet. I was putting my boots back on when a car's headlights looked like they were almost on top of me. I tried to get out of the way, but it was too late. The impact was so powerful that it lifted me up in the air.

"They killed my son! Angel, Martín is dead!"

"He's not dead. Look, he's still breathing. Martín, we're almost there. Michoacano, check his pulse."

I have no idea how much time transpired. I opened my eyes, and I saw my father, sitting on the ground, bowing his head, his hands covering his face. The Angel and the man from Michoacan were staring at me closely. My father started to laugh and cry at the same time. He hugged me. It hurt to be embraced.

"All I could think about was what was I going to tell your mother," he told me.

He couldn't stop crying. The Angel and the man from Michoacan both helped me back to my feet. I noticed that I was barefoot: the collision had knocked the boots right off my feet. My head and my hip hurt, too. We started walking again, this time more slowly than before. Supporting myself at times on my father, then on The Angel, the pain in my hip began to diminish.

The Angel tried to cheer me up. "Don't worry. We're almost there."

We crossed over roads and through thickets; we went up and down the highways. Whenever we saw a police car, we would hide in the bushes. They terrified me because I didn't know there was a difference between the police and the Border Patrol.

We walked from San Bernardino to Los Angeles. The hour and a half that The Angel had told me about was the distance by car. On foot, it took much longer. Seeing the city lights gave us new hope.

"There won't be any more problems once we get to El Monte," The Angel said.

We continued to walk, but I couldn't see the mound of dirt that was supposed to be the sign that we were out of danger.

"You really are a dummy, aren't you? El Monte is the name of the city," The Angel told me.

In El Monte, The Angel took us to a bus station. We entered the main lobby; everyone was looking at us as if we were ghosts. Our darkened faces, our chapped lips, almost white, our filthy clothes, our starved bellies. I looked at the man from Michoacan; his eyes were expressionless. It was as if he had grown accustomed to not eating, not sleeping, not thinking. He had not complained once during the entire journey. We stayed at the water fountain for a long time; we took turns taking drinks. We drank water until we got our fill.

We had no money for the bus. My father removed a crumpled envelope that he had kept in his pants. It was a letter that contained the address of a lady friend of my mother's. She was the manager of a little hotel in Los Angeles, but my mother had received the letter many years ago. We didn't know if we were going to be able to find her.

The Angel told us to beg for the money that we needed for our bus fare. It was the first time that my father and I had ever asked for money from a stranger, but we did it. After about an hour, we were able to collect two dollars, precisely how much we needed to get to Los Angeles.

We got on the bus. I pressed my face against the window. It was the first time I had seen so many new cars all on the same road. The bus passed them with ease. My father showed the address to The Angel, who went up to the bus driver and instructed him to drop us off on a street corner downtown. "Your stop is not far from the hotel," he told us.

I looked at The Angel out of the corner of my eye. He was like a shadow. His lips full, his eyebrows straight, and his eyes fixed on a distant point. He was a hero. Thanks to him, we didn't get crushed on the train tracks. People walked by without taking notice of him. "Look at him. He's a hero," I thought to myself. His farewell was brief, almost impersonal: "We're gonna stay on all the way down to Huntington Park."

The Angel was right; the hotel was nearby.

On the way, we thought about what we would do if we couldn't find my mother's friend. Without knowing a soul, without knowing where to go or where to begin, we knocked on the door. Fortunately for us, my mother's friend was there to receive us. The introductions were brief; there was no need for explanations. She escorted us through a hallway and showed us to our room. There was only one bed. We didn't wake up until the following day.

I opened my eyes. I tried to get up, but I couldn't.

My father tried to comfort me, "You can't get up, can you? Me neither."

It was as if someone had been pounding on our legs all night long. We examined our calves. It looked like a field of giant mushrooms, covered by the skin of our calves. There wasn't a single spot on our legs that didn't have some sort of protuberance. We started to massage ourselves frantically. The pain I felt when I took my first step forced tears from my eyes. Perhaps it was exactly the pretext I needed to get the weight off my shoulders from all of the horrors I had experienced over the course of my journey. We didn't leave our room for two whole days. My mother's friend brought us food on two separate occasions. She lent us an ointment to reduce the inflammation.

On the third day, my father went to get a copy of the newspaper in order to look for work. There was an article printed in great, big letters:

> Mexico's economic recovery falters. Corruption discovered at PEMEX. Corporate leaders also accused of using company employees to work on their own private estates.

"Nothing's going to change in Mexico. We did the right thing by coming here," my father said.

In the first week he went to look for work, they gave my father a shift at one of the factories. It took me longer; I was seventeen, but looked fifteen.

I didn't cry when I first left home; the idea of going to the United States was so attractive to me. I didn't cry when I said good-bye to my mother either. But I'm crying now. The tears are flowing, and there's no way to stop them. I don't want to stop them. It's as if by telling my story, I've been made to live it all over again. I cry out of sadness for all of those who now cross the border in a thousand different ways, but I also cry for joy because I made it alive. I married a girl from Jalisco. I have three beautiful children. A good job. I'm going to become a citizen very soon. I tell you all of this so that those who are already here in the United States do not mislead those who are still in Mexico. The road is hard, very hard. God bears witness to how hard it truly is.

Martín
Los Angeles, California

My Name Is Pedro Infante and He's . . . Jorge Negrete

Carlos, my brother-in-law, at every opportunity, strove to be extra friendly with me. He was my only sister's boyfriend. She was about to finish high school and, like any good student, would soon be off to college. Carlos was a bricklayer. My parents were never very happy about this relationship; I liked it even less. The last straw was when he took her away from us, just a few days after my sister's graduation. He rode off with her—on his bicycle! They got married, and poverty overwhelmed them as unemployment continued to grow. She was left frustrated: her education cut short, her life, her poverty, and all that at just sixteen years of age.

A friend invited me to go to Los Angeles. A work contractor had offered us jobs. The idea was to cross the border in Tijuana. I talked Carlos into going with me. I interceded on his behalf to my sister, convincing her that it was the best thing to do. She agreed. I set a date for our departure: the end of July 1994. My goal was to get him away from her. His, to be successful! Since we weren't too poorly dressed, we pretended to be members of the Legislative Committee sent to investigate the Luis Donaldo Colosio assassination, and we were able to get a couple of bus tickets. We saved fifty percent on travel expenses. At 10:50 at night, we boarded the bus to Guadalajara; and, at around twelve o'clock, we reached the Periférico highway surrounding the city and then transferred to a bus destined for Tijuana. Everything was going as planned.

We arrived at the border at daybreak. A taxi took us to find accommodations near the shop belonging to the friend who had invited us. On the following morning, we showed up as soon as it opened for business. He had been expecting us because we had spoken to him over the telephone. Our friend took us out for breakfast, and while we were eating, I told him what we were planning to do. I let him in on our plans to go up North. He thought it was a harebrained idea, especially because he knew that I didn't have a passport and that his relative, the "pollero" who was supposed to help us across, had recently been arrested, thus eliminating the only trustworthy contact we had in order to "jump over the border." Nevertheless, our enthusiasm had not subsided. We looked in downtown Tijuana for someone who could cross us, but no one wanted to charge less than a thousand dollars. There was no way that we could afford to pay that much, because we only had a little bit of money.

Someone told us that a lot of people passed along the Tijuana beaches. My brother-in-law and I went there, and we saw how the "coyotes" organized everybody, shouting at them:

"Don't wear any light-colored shirts. . . ."

"Hey, only one bottle of water . . ."

"No baseball caps . . ."

"Take two changes of dark clothing. . . ."

"Tennis shoes, only tennis shoes . . ."

There were three polleros. They divided the contingent into groups, one to each side with his own group, and the one on top of the border fence who, by way of coded whistling, communicated with the others. One whistle meant for group one to run; two whistles, group two followed; a long whistle, everyone ducked or retreated.

"I'll get you across!" I told Carlos.

He just laughed while I called myself a *cabrón*. I went to the swapmeet on the corner of Fifth and Tenth; there we bought the appropriate shoes and clothing. We ate, then left to share our plan with my friend. He practically chained us up to prevent us from going through with it. He could not convince us to stay. We entrusted him with our luggage and our money so that he could send them to us on the other side once we were able to cross over. Everything was set.

We arrived at the beach at four in the afternoon. There were only a few others . . . and all of them frightened. I climbed up onto the fence just as I had seen the coyote do it. I got the lay of the land; I spotted the Border Patrol; I got a fix on their positions; I calculated their line of sight from that distance; I mapped out our trajectory; and in approximately two minutes' time, I screamed excitedly, "I've got it! Let's go!"

Through a hole beneath the fence, we let ourselves roll down onto a hollow; a trail of really fine, deep, white sand followed. We paused for a moment. Our deep footprints could leave evidence of our steps. Since I had been a Boy Scout, I took a dry branch, and wiggling backwards and going back and forth with the branch, I covered our tracks, like the Apaches did. Right then, we heard a noise; we ran and took cover behind a shrub. A truck drove by. We remained very still for a moment; then, on the count of three, we ran like a hundred-meter dash through the brambles and crags, on our way to the beach. There was a little ditch filled with rattan and bulrush where we crossed the border headed toward San Diego. Suddenly, we heard a noise: "¡El mosco! (The Border Patrol helicopter)." And, zoom, we threw ourselves into a puddle of water, covering ourselves up with underbrush. The key was not to break the reeds, for they would surely recognize the trail left behind us from above . . . and that's what we did on two or three occasions until we couldn't hear anything anymore. In front of us, there was a span of about fifty yards separating us from a wall of bamboo trees that paralleled the border fence that we had left behind. To our left, we could see the beach and the ocean; to our right, there were Border Patrol vehicles. I chose to spy on the Border Patrol; we were drenched with fear as much as with the sweat that ran down our foreheads and dampened our backs.

Carlos and I rolled onto our sides, little by little, until we reached a grove of trees that would provide us with some camouflage. We spotted another road; it was sandy. It appeared to be exactly like the one we had just crossed. Before determining where the other road would lead us, we decided to rest. That previous "Rambo" scene had made us break a sweat, accelerate our heart rate, and secrete adrenaline by the boatload. We were barely beginning to catch our breath when, in the distance, we spotted the Border Patrol! To our right, a patrol car with its lights on headed in our direction. On the other side, there was a small booth dividing the two lanes of the road. We watched carefully from our hiding place. The squad car started in our direction. When it came across another police vehicle, the two drivers greeted one another, and the one that was coming toward us followed the other patrol. We realized that there were a lot of them and that they drove around in circles along the same route. It occurred to me that between their sightings and greetings, we could very easily advance to the little booth, and that's what we did. We made it. But it was empty! Suddenly, in the intersection, passing before our very eyes were a number of men on horseback; we remained still. They were American ranchers who greeted us when they saw us.

They continued on like nothing, maybe even wishing us luck. Lying down, we continued to roll with our heads turned towards the patrol car, praying to God that they would become distracted or that their longrange vision would only detect a small ball rolling on the ground. In a single bound, we were able to reach a patch of grass that protected us from being seen. Then, after a light jog, we came to a six-foot-wide canal full of pestilent mud, and this was our next obstacle. We could clearly hear the helicopters circling over our heads: they were going around and around.

We awaited the next encounter. I ran, pushed myself, jumped, and fell into the canal, sinking slowly. Carlos didn't move. But I could see how the grass shook with his laughter. He waited until the helicopters passed by and then jumped to the other bank, using me to support his foot. All spiffy clean, he searched for a branch; he held it out for me; and, pulled me out . . . Pee-yew! I smelled awful!

Beneath a tree, we found dry but dirty clothes; perhaps those who had passed by that same spot had left them behind. We looked for things to wear. We left our clothes, putting on different pairs of pants and shirts that were two sizes too big. The field that awaited us had no foliage to provide us with cover; we saw a mound of trees in the distance, and we ran nonstop until we reached it. Suddenly, we spotted another helicopter.

"That mosco saw us!" screamed Carlos.

The helicopter descended upon us; the air from its propellers rustled the branches that were covering us. Curled up into protruding little bundles, I believed that the object underneath the helicopter was some sort of heat or movement detector, and that, its sensor would detect a mere rabbit or some other kind of small animal. My nervousness prevented me from hearing precisely what was being said over the helicopter's loudspeaker. Cries and screams could be heard; there was a mad dash by some of the people who all of a sudden ran out from their hidings. We were not alone! The din grew further away, perhaps in pursuit of those in the trees.

We decided to walk through a riverbed that had some shallow pools of water or traces of moisture in only a few spots, but was full of insects. We walked inside of it for about thirty minutes and then decided to go out and see where we were going. A noise to our right helped us to find a coyote who was barely poking his nose over a rock in order to get the lay of the land. I went up to him, perhaps without taking the necessary precautions. I was able to see him clearly in spite of the haze: his round face, his runny eyes, his broad nose breathing heavily. He scolded me. Frightened, he indicated to me that we couldn't keep going at that time; it was better to wait until night had fallen. When it got dark, hundreds of gigantic floodlights illuminated the only road, which now looked like a bridge, though, to me, due to fear and our circumstances, it appeared to be more like a giant catwalk for a Miss Universe pageant. I couldn't wait any longer; Carlos and I started a mad dash straight ahead, with all of our nervous energy focused on turning ourselves into gazelles. And wham! I slammed my side on a jagged rock that cut a gash over the rib above my right hip. When Carlos saw me go down, he stopped a few yards ahead of me: he was an athlete. We rolled into the grass on the side of the path. My wound bled profusely, and the pain was unbearable. Nevertheless, I insisted that Carlos and I continue as soon as the helicopter and its blinding spot light flew over our hiding place. We had to duck down again near the side of the road on two or three occasions, whenever the police vehicles drove close by, but we would quickly get back on the path as soon as we could.

The first house in town, after the farms, was our destination; it had no gate. It had a beautiful garden, and in the middle of a cypress trees, under a window, we found a water hose that we used to bathe and to wash our clothes. We combed our hair. We did everything in parts, because the patrols were regular and incessant, until a "gringo" neighbor shouted, "Hey! What are you doing?" Carlos didn't say a thing; he just began to walk away as he called me over. I went after him, still only half dressed. I caught up to him further ahead, and pretending to converse in English, we blended in with other people, trying to go about it naturally, even though we were stinky and wet. A helicopter passed by, and its light shone upon us. It forced us to go into a house. We did it as if it were our own, but when the lights came on outside the house, it scared us even more. The searchlight passed by, and sneaking away, we continued our journey.

A short, dark-skinned man leaning on his doorway observed us. We went up to him and asked for clothing, and he offered to provide us with a change of clothes, instructing us to keep walking until we reached the park, where there were more "wetbacks." Many blocks down the road, he caught up to us with the clothes. He refused the money that we offered him. We changed in somebody's yard. The new clothes were too small but they were clean. We finished fixing ourselves up in the park: no more mud on our shoes and our hair was perfectly in place.

At a gas station, they told us where to go next. We had to take the trolley. Our next obstacle was that we only had Mexican money on us, and it wasn't exactly the right time to go to a money exchange booth or to a bank; and besides, we weren't really sure how to make the transaction. Luckily, outside of the store that sold the tickets for the trolley, a Mexican couple, realizing the situation we were in, exchanged just enough of our money for us to buy the tickets. Carlos and I sat far back of the very last car just in case something happened. This position, we thought, would give us enough time to take notice and try to run away. Nothing happened.

We saw the trolley stations as they went by, and we kept track of them on the maps located on the trolley car walls, we had to get off at the Santa Fe train depot. It was ten o'clock at night when we got off, it was time to sleep. Luckily, there were a lot of hotels in the area. We chose the one nearest to the train station, and we made ourselves at home in its garden. Between the shrubs on the path, next to the sidewalk, a copy of the *Watchtower* (a Jehovah Witness magazine) served as our shelter. It was five o'clock in the morning when the sound of the cars woke me up.

Carlos and I went to the station right as a freight train was leaving. We hopped on the train. It traveled parallel to the trolley tracks, and I noticed the names of the stations we had seen the night before. We were going the wrong way! We jumped off and retraced our steps on the tracks for approximately one hour, until we saw three Mexicans underneath a bridge who were putting their clothes on in a hurry, as if they had just finished having sex. One of them proved to be friendly, though somewhat embarrassed that we had walked in on them. He warned us not to trespass on federal property.

"They can arrest you. Did you just make it across?" he asked.

"Yeah, last night," I answered.

"And I suppose you haven't eaten yet, right? Look, go on over to the mission. That big house with an orange-and-green-tiled roof. They give out bread and coffee at seven. So get going!"

We headed in the mission's direction. There was already a line of about a hundred people, all in need: blacks, a lot of whites, and a few Spanish-speakers. We approached a group of them. There was a Cuban, whose dental plaque came out every time he talked; a blond-haired Salvadoran whom they referred to as "Cristo" because he looked like Jesus Christ; a short and skinny black Nicaraguan with some really big headphones and a very stylish haircut; there was also a Mexican who looked like Rafael Inclán (a Mexican comedian) and bragged about stealing cars. We joined up with them; we talked, and they advised us on how to continue on to Los Angeles. From the bread-and-coffee place, we then followed them to another mission, where we could take a bath at eight o'clock. There was already a line, and they hadn't even opened yet. Inside, they gave out shampoo and soap; and, with an I. D., one could even receive a towel and a comb. The only bad thing was that there were dozens of showers in an open, communal space. We all had to shower together!

The big surprise was the huge size of those black guys' members. Holy cow! Their reputation was justified. I asked Carlos if we could alternate our turns in the shower to protect each other in case one of us dropped the soap. We didn't want to risk an assault on our integrity.

Now that we were all cleaned up, we needed clothes. Inclán and Cristo took us to a flea market so that we could exchange our pesos for dollars. From there, they showed us to a secondhand clothing store, where even they got all "fancied up."

We returned to the mission where the lawns served as tanning beds for all of the poor people. We lay out next to a friendly, young and chubby white girl whom they called "Cat"; she spoke some choppy but intelligible Spanish. She offered us night jobs: selling drugs! Outside the mission, there were vendors of every color selling pills, pot, crystal, and crack cocaine!

Carlos went inside to explore the interior of the mission; it even had a lobby and reading rooms. I continued gallivanting about, when a police car stopped in front of the door and two young officers dressed in civilian clothes descended from their vehicle. They questioned us: Cat, me, and a "cholo" with multiple tattoos of the number 18—one of the most feared gangs in Los Angeles. They checked his record, and he cried like a baby; he wasn't more than nineteen years old. He swore that it had to be some kind of mistake. They dragged him off against his will.

Carlos came out laughing along with Cristo, who had told him that we should leave on the following day. Until then, we had to find a place to sleep. The solution: another mission in San Diego, a Protestant one, of course. They said there weren't any Catholic ones. We had to stand in line on the sidewalk for three hours in front of the new mission; they opened precisely at seven o'clock and only for a few minutes.

While waiting, some handsome, finely dressed American men in expensive automobiles parked in front of us. They looked us over thoroughly until someone bold enough approached them. They said something, then he got into the car; and an hour later they came back with the guy all cleaned up, providing him with some new clothes, brand-name tennis shoes, and perhaps a little money for his pockets.

Brazen and bejeweled, one of the American men walked up to us. He directed his steps toward Carlos, telling him, "You're suffering because you want to suffer. You're a handsome guy and don't even have to work, because I can take care of you. All you'll have to do is sit around the house all day, and we'll just take it easy all night long."

His comments provoked malicious laughter from everybody. I said to Carlos, "Don't even worry about me. Go for it."

His face turned beet red. He declined the invitation. It was finally seven o'clock and the mission was opened. We went into a large auditorium-like room. It looked like a church. We participated in the ceremony with our praying, singing, shouting, and clapping. Next to me, a smelly guy who we nicknamed "Pigpen," a good friend of the group that we were running with, listened to music on his headphones while his body grooved. A man approached him: "Brother, out of respect, if they're going to feed you dinner, and if you can't understand what they're saying, you can at least applaud. But don't dance around like that."

At around nine o'clock, dinner was served. They gave us a lot to eat. A fat black man, lounging behind a desk, was in charge of registration and distribution of the lodgings. Cristo encouraged us to go up to him and, along with some others, they took us in with the warning that it would only be for a single night. We exchanged our dirty clothes for clean ones, they even gave us shoes. Right after, we took an obligatory bath and then went to bed in hospital gowns. The portable beds were comfortable, and the place was very clean and excessively tidy. We were even able to ask them to wake us up early in order to catch our train. They got us up at exactly six o'clock on the following morning. A courteous and discreet Anglo man woke us up. As soon as we were ready, he directed us to an enormous dining hall where we had a hearty breakfast, consisting of vegetables, pancakes, coffee, and milk. From there, we went out into the dark street outside. But, oh no, we were wrong about the itinerary! At the station, we learned that the train to Los Angeles didn't leave until 11 o'clock in the morning. We went back and had some coffee. We found ourselves among the group that, always punctual, occupies the first places in line. We went inside, and from there a line started that went out into the street and started to stretch out the length of the block. We were chitchatting when a big commotion outside of the mission made us look up to see what was going on. It was the Border Patrol interrogating everyone as they exited the building.

We didn't know what to do. It was too late to start running. We would give ourselves away. Panic was written all over Carlos's face. The security guard insisted that we move on. The line continued to advance. Once a person had been served, with his plate in hand, he had to leave. That's why we decided to go back to the end of the line again. The third time that we did it, the security guard came up to us. I thought he was going to turn us in. The Border Patrol officers were only a few yards away. They continued to question people and demand documentation from those who were exiting. There were only two people in front of us, then it was our turn. We couldn't go to the end of the line again: the security guard was watching us. I saw myself in handcuffs and Carlos resigned at my side. I wanted to pray, but I couldn't remember any prayers. We were next. Then, at that very moment, a miracle occurred! The officers left without detaining anybody. We had lost our appetites due to the fright, and our stomachs wreaked havoc upon us. We put down our trays and went to the bathroom, then we went out to the garden. I lay down next to a group of black girls with plunging necklines, and in my limited English, I tried to flirt with them. One of them came up to me. I caressed her intimate body parts; she did the same to me. Her hair awakened a curiosity within me. I touched it. Like a spiral, her bristly hair curled around my fingers. She offered herself to me in exchange for a soda. I didn't even have enough money for that.

The following morning, we located the freight train, and when it departed, we waited a few blocks ahead of it to hitch a ride. We started to race toward it. It was dangerous. A fall could take one of our legs, or maybe even our lives. Nevertheless, I hopped on. But Carlos didn't! I had to jump off. I was annoyed by his indecision. We had to call the work contractor, the brother of our host in Tijuana, in order to make him aware of the setback. It was now too late to go eat breakfast, so we went back to the black girls. Before we arrived, a fat black man, standing by his shiny truck, said something to us. Mumbling my reply, I refused his invitation.

"Do you want to give us some work?" asked Carlos.

He concurred, and we agreed to go with him in his truck. We had to put up a wooden fence on the side of his house, dig holes, install iron poles and cement them in, in order to brace the staves of redwood from them. The four hours of labor were doubled because the materials hadn't arrived yet. The generous boss treated us to plenty of grilled hotdogs and cold sodas. After we had finished, he paid us forty dollars each. We were rich! We embarked on our trek back to the mission to get some sleep. We signed in with different names, and once again, they took us in. We attended the "religious extravaganza." Shouts, cries, sermons, and applause. The converts were allowed to stay and live inside the mission with some assistance and some monetary compensation. We almost did it. Spiritually, we felt reborn. Carlos spoke to me about my sister. The separation made him sadder and sadder. We walked out into the garden. On the grass, covered with a blanket, out where everyone could see, a couple was having sex. Further away, other people were doing drugs.

Cristo had the telephone number of a place where they helped people who were having difficulty getting back to Los Angeles. He called and, in good English, lied that his car had broken down on the freeway. He told them that he needed to return to Los Angeles to be with his family. They gave him an address. We went over there. When we arrived, we filled out some forms. A very friendly black pastor interviewed us. He gave us money for the bus, and he handed us a piece of paper with instructions about where to get on and where to get off and how to use the bus transfers. He also gave us a sack full of canned food.

We boarded the first bus in downtown San Diego, destined for La Jolla; but, unsure how to use the transfers and unfamiliar with the exact itineraries, we wasted some money and missed a lot of buses. Before getting on the bus to Oceanside, we lunched on the canned food that we had brought with us. We got to Oceanside, then boarded the next bus that went through Camp Pendleton. Something else that we were unaware of was that at the entrance to the military base, a marine would step on the bus, saying, "Papers . . . Papers . . ."

They detained us. They asked us our personal information and handcuffed us. We gave them Mexico's most well known singer's names—Jorge Negrete and Pedro Infante—for our names. The Border Patrol vehicle would be arriving in a matter of minutes. I pleaded with the marine who held us in custody. I begged him and told him about everything we had gone through to make it that far. I asked him just to let us go on the sly. He listened to me in silence. His gaze had ceased to be so piercing and cold. He went up to the desk. He peeked out the window. He took out the key to the handcuffs. He looked at us with compassion. I listened to Carlos's heavy breathing. He was going to set us free.

"I can't let you guys go. I already reported you to immigration," he said regretfully.

I kept on insisting. He apologized for not being able to help us. "The Border Patrol should be here soon."

We would not resign ourselves to being deported. I tried to free my wrists from the metal that bound them, but I only got up to half of my right palm, really hurting myself, without any favorable results. Carlos, on the other hand, had already freed one of his hands and showed it to me with a feeling of satisfaction. Quickly, I told him to hide it back behind his body, while I tried to distract the marine. I moved next to Carlos so that he could remove the maps, directions, and money from my pockets. The idea was for him to get to

Los Angeles, even if he went alone. After pointing out the train that passed right in front of the base, I got up from my seat, and I walked back up to the marine again; I struck up some trivial conversation about the pictures of the generals that adorned the walls of the room. He went on telling me, one by one, about their lives' trials and tribulations. . . . We were so entertained that I don't even know when Carlos got out of there. The Border Patrol officers arrived, one of them an Oriental. Two illegals had been reported, but they saw only one. They asked for an explanation, raising their voices and demanding answers from the marine. Another officer arrived. I was only able to say "what?" to his questions.

They arrested the marine, and, in a Glory Halleluiah, a horde of marines appeared; they even came in jeeps. It was like a scene from a Rambo movie. They searched everywhere.

An older officer, all-smiles, questioned me in a very friendly way. He spoke to me about the danger Carlos was in: "They might confuse him with an assassin and shoot at him."

I didn't rule out the possibility, but I stood firm. They put me in a Border Patrol Blazer, and the old man started to call out to him over the loudspeaker, "Jorge Negrete! Come out! Your friend Pedro Infante is here . . . Come on out! It's mooey peligrosouh for you out there. . . ."

He passed me the loudspeaker so that I could try to convince him to turn himself in. I was able to yell, "Run! Run . . . You made it!"

He snatched the apparatus away from me violently. He was very upset with me. We went back to the place where the marines were searching. Almost four hours had gone by when they showed up with Carlos, who, between snickers, told me how he had taken off his boxers and was able to cover up the handcuffs stuck to his forearm with them in the form of a bandage. He had climbed a tree, and from there he observed the whole mobilization of marines and Border

Patrol officers. He waited until they had moved some distance away. He left his hiding place to seek refuge in a drainage tube near the freeway and waited for the bus there. When he saw it approaching, he was able to board without any problems, but they caught him at the San Clemente checkpoint and then sent him back to the marine base. We were back together again. The Border Patrol took us to a detention facility where they waited for more wetbacks. A Tex-Mexican made us clean the bus from "head to tail." He let us eat as many cookies and drink as much juice as we wanted to until we were full. It was midnight by the time we got to Tijuana.

"Are you going to try it again?" asked the officer from Texas.

"Yeah. First thing tomorrow," I replied.

He bid us farewell with a slap on the back, wishing us luck. The sun was beginning to rise when we hailed a taxi that took us to downtown. From there I called my friend, who told us how to get to his house. A couple of tequila shots got us singing. We went to bed early. When we woke up, my friend had already gone to his office. We headed down toward the market on Francisco Villa. We were ready to start our journey all over again. This time we made sure to exchange enough money. We passed through the fence, through the hole, racing, over the roads, through the junkyards, through the walls of trees, across the smelly canal; but this time, we wore two changes of clothes, we didn't care about getting dirty; like a pair of snakes, we shed our skin under a tree . . . through the riverbed, over the bridge, into the town, taking the trolley to San Diego. We arrived late at the mission, so we had to sleep out on the street, behind some banana trees. We were covered with newspapers, very close to the mission that served coffee, which is where we went very early the next morning. We greeted all the regulars. The group of Latinos joked about our speedy return. The laughter turned into hilarity when we told them about what had happened to us. Tired, Carlos decided to accept Inclán's proposition to contract a coyote for $500.

I opted to take the bus route. I filled a bottle with water and got on the bus before anyone else so that I could pour water on the backseats from the exit door all the way to the back of the bus. I sealed off that section with Scotch tape from which I hung a sign saying: "Don't trespass." The sign fell down, and two people walked by it. I convinced the first one by begging him in *pikinglish* to sit closer to the front, but I couldn't convince the second guy. Finally, minutes before the bus made its stop at the San Clemente checkpoint, the second guy took pity on me and moved to a front seat.

I put the sign back up in its place, and I was barely able to dive down between the seats and the right-hand wall of the bus. When the marine boarded the bus and saw that the back section was empty, he didn't even bother to look. The bus followed its route. I came out from my hiding place, grateful to my unusual accomplices. I found a pair of sandals under the seat I had used to hide; I suppose they had belonged to one of those surfer boys that got on the bus near the beach. I put them on in order to appear to be another one of them, so as not to give rise to any suspicions that I might be a wetback.

It was nighttime when we finally reached Los Angeles. Luckily, a Mexican who got off an hour before I did offered to assist me. I asked him to call the work contractor and tell him to wait for me on the corner of Seventh and Main. It was where my index finger fell on the map. I missed the stop where I was supposed to get off; the bus driver gave me a transfer to go back. I called the contractor on his cellular from César Chávez. Thirty minutes later, an expensive truck drove up to me. A young, light-skinned guy with a full beard rolled down the window of the right door and asked my name. Happily, I asked him his own. During the drive, I realized that he had a number of firearms with him. He explained that the neighborhood was a "very hot" place, full of gangsters and people up to no good. By the following day, I was working for him.

Meanwhile, Carlos was still unable to pass through the San Clemente checkpoint. On a number of occasions, the guys who sent him back to Tijuana were the same ones who kept catching him. In the end, he was finally able to make it across. They handed him over to me in Long Beach. I paid the coyote with the money I had earned, and we had enough left over to celebrate. We were pleased with our arrival in "The Land of Opportunity."

After four years, a lot of work, and not much fun, Carlos returned to Mexico. With the money he had saved, he was able to buy a house for my sister and a car for himself. I've gone back and forth about three times, always giving the Border Patrol the slip. If things continue to be like this in Mexico, more Mexicans will be sure to do the same.

Ulises
Pacoima, California

Some Nachos to Go

In Jalpa, Zacatecas, just like in all the other towns in Mexico, on every September sixteenth, an Independence Day parade follows the El Grito de la Independencia ceremony. On this national holiday, my mother and my aunt got together to buy me an airplane ticket to Los Angeles.

I said good-bye to my grandfather, not knowing if I'd ever see him again. He gave me his blessing, and before I left, he gave me all the savings that he had put aside. With his hard, dry, stone-like fingers, he untied the knot in his red bandanna and counted out the money: twenty-five pesos. It was enough to buy me a bus ticket to Guadalajara. My grandfather didn't want to accompany me to the bus station. "Go with your friend, Rosi," he told me.

There was a party going on in Jalpa. Houses, shops, stores, government buildings—everything was draped with Mexican flags. People were already making themselves comfortable along the streets to watch the parade. Every year, all over the country, people celebrate with parades and drunkenness the day when Mexico won its independence from Spain.

Long crepe-paper chains in the colors of the flag—green, white and red—adorned the entrances to the government buildings. I felt a great deal of resentment. I was a member of the Catholic youth movement. In my youth group, they preached kindness, love, respect, and moral and material support for those in need. However, in the midst of so many good intentions, no one could provide me with a job. They spoke of charity, but no one offered me any help. I had grown up with the firm belief that material possessions would be my reward for honesty, integrity, and hard work. Nothing turned out that way. My grandfather ended up losing his land, and I was forced to emigrate to another country in order to live. I had applied to my life the contents of the prayers that I recited by heart on every first Friday of the month in front of the group. I was proud of having done so. Repeating them over and over again lightened the burden of the sadness that I felt upon parting with my grandfather: *Lord, I believe in Thee: increase my faith. I trust in Thee: strengthen my trust. I love Thee: let me love Thee more and more. I am sorry for my sins: deepen my sorrow. I worship Thee as my first beginning, I long for Thee as my last end; I praise Thee as my constant helper, and call on Thee as my loving protector. Guide me by Thy wisdom, correct me with Thy justice, comfort me with Thy mercy, protect me with Thy power. I offer Thee, Lord, my thoughts; to be fixed on Thee; my words: to have Thee for their theme; my actions: to reflect my love for Thee; my sufferings: to be endured for Thy greater glory. I want to do what Thou asketh of me: in the way Thou asketh, because Thou asketh. Lord, enlighten my understanding, strengthen my will, purify my heart, and make me holy. Help me to repent of my past sins and to resist temptation in the future. Help me to rise above my human weakness and to grow stronger as a Christian. Let me love Thee, my Lord and my God, and see myself as I really am: a pilgrim in this world, a Christian called to respect and love all whose lives I touch, those in authority over me or those under my authority, my friends and my enemies. Help me to conquer anger with gentleness, greed with generosity, apa-*

thy with fervor. Help me to forget myself and reach out toward others. Make me prudent in planning, courageous in taking risks. Make me patient in suffering, unassuming in prosperity. Keep me, Lord, attentive at prayer, temperate in food and drink, diligent in my work, firm in my good intentions. Let my conscience be clear, my conduct without fault, my speech blameless, my life well-ordered. Put me on guard against my human weaknesses. Let me cherish Thy love for me, keep Thy law, and come at last to Thy salvation. Grant me this, oh Lord . . . Grant me this, oh Lord . . . Grant me this, oh Lord . . .

The same thing would always happen to me with that last part. I would suddenly forget how it ended. Perhaps because it spoke of death. In the end, I would improvise my own conclusion. My friends never seemed to notice, but Father Jacinto, the one who presided over the group, had also memorized every word of the *Oratio Universalis* written by Pope Clement XI.

My prayers granted me a great deal of peace, but they didn't resolve my problems. The money that my mom sent to me from Los Angeles covered less and less of what I needed to stay in school, without the slightest hope of enrolling in a university. The only solution was to join her in the United States, study English, and find a job. That way we would be able to help my grandfather get out of debt. He had lost his land a year before. It never rained that year, and his credit overwhelmed him. El Banco Ejidal, the farm loan bank, would not take responsibility; and along with another group of *ejido* farmers, they all wanted to lynch the bank manager.

Coming around the corner of the bank, a group of students in starched uniforms—the boys wearing white shirts and slacks and the girls in blue blazers and skirts—prepared to get the parade under way. Some carried trombones and others clarinets. They rehearsed the National Anthem of Mexico. Hearing the anthem filled me with emotion; but at the same, it added to my resentment.

The nearby church bells struck eight o'clock. I still had two hours before I had to take my bus. Calmly, I continued to watch the uniformed boys and girls, who, on the order of "double-time . . . march!" advanced. I saw myself among their ranks. "One, two, one, one, one, two . . . ready . . . halt!" They stopped at the street corner. I absorbed the images. I wanted to carry them with me intact. The students had covered their hands with colorful ribbons.

I didn't want to leave. The parade had begun. There were entire families sitting all along the sidewalk. Some brought benches to sit; others laid out mattresses on the edge of the sidewalk. They sat their children in a row. "Look at the pretty ribbons." The contingent of students marched on. The military band played again. The girls moved their arms in different directions. The ribbons made whimsical shapes in the wind. The people applauded. The roving venders announced, "Come get your tacos here! Tacos with brains, intestines, or steak!" More people continued to arrive. Some paid no attention to the parade. "Put a lot of chile on my corn-on-the-cob, please." "Go get the guy with the cotton candy." "Hold the onions on my *torta*." The students at the head of the parade were now far ahead. I checked my watch. I walked quickly. Rosi's house was close to the plaza.

Rosi was already waiting for me at the door. Solemn, mysterious, she never wanted to go with me to the Catholic youth group. "The church is as much to blame as the government for things being so screwed up for us," my friend had told me many times.

From the time that we were in middle school, her position had been to reject all established institutions. "That bunch of crooks," which is what my mom also called the government, "was the one who left your grandfather without any land. And now, look: you have to leave. It's just not fair," she said almost to herself.

She had platinum blonde hair and near metallic blue eyes. She had a little pug nose, and her lips were very full, well-defined, and they never stopped moving, making way for the words that came rushing out. "You should be happy that you're leaving this place where the only thing that matters are contacts and connections. And forget about all of those buttheads in church who spend all their time praying and preaching about love and charity, because when they see you starving to death on the sidewalk, they just kick you out of the way. You'll be better off on the other side."

Her words sounded cold, almost glacial, to me. I took her by the arm. A profound silence followed. I broke it by promising her that I would be back in two months.

"You're never coming back. What would you be coming back to? Even Divine Providence has forsaken this place." I was shocked by her deductions and analysis.

The bus station was little more than a provisional street corner where the bus came along bearing a sign reading "Guadalajara." Rosi helped me to board the bus. I watched her through the window: standing tall, wiping away her tears with a closed fist. I couldn't contain myself. I jumped off the bus again, and ran to her and gave her a hug. We both cried. Our sorrow was expressed in a moan, a sob. We cried for Jalpa, for the tranquil, tearful fields that surrounded us as girls, for the gilded and azure afternoons, for the bitterness of distance. We reached out our hands and promised to write each other every week.

I got back on the bus and took my seat. As a devout Catholic, I shouldn't have felt worried: "God will provide," Father Jacinto had said so many times. But God only provided for a select few: the politicians and their families. They owned the big houses; they controlled the rivers that passed through the fields. Perhaps Rosi was right: "Divine Providence had forsaken Jalpa."

I closed my eyes. The smell of guayaba filtered through the bus windows. A light rain began to dampen the city streets. A sudden hate welled up inside of me. My heart burst with rage against those who had everything. I moaned, I cried, and I talked to myself. Many desolate hours awaited me. The contradictions were turning the world upside down in my head. The bus opened up a path through the middle of an exuberant abundance. Enormous cultivated fields. Trees full of fruit. Like weather vanes, the parabolic antennae pointed in the direction of our destination. How could there be such wealth and at the same time so much misery in my beloved Mexico?

At the station, I waited for another bus that would take me to the airport. The rumble of the crowds frightened away my sorrow. I had never seen so many buses together in one place. It was my first time flying on an airplane, and all I knew was that I would be leaving on an Aeromexico flight headed for Los Angeles. The grumbling in my belly reminded me that I hadn't eaten breakfast, and it was already past lunchtime.

Someone had mounted a poster on a wall with information about Guadalajara:

> *Encyclopedia of Mexico.* Volume 5. Guadalajara (An Arabic word meaning "River of Stones") is the capital of the state of Jalisco. After Mexico City, it is the federal entity with the highest population and the greatest amount of commercial, industrial, and service-oriented activity. The city is bordered to the north by the San Isidro mesa, to the south by the Cuatro, Santa María, and Gachupín mountains, to the east by the suburb of Tonalá, and to the west by the Venta mountain range. At the end of the pre-Hispanic period, the Cocas,

Tecuexes and Caxcanes all lived in the Guadalajara valley. These groups disappeared without leaving a trace. Bands of the Quinametzin, the corpulent men who founded Teotihuacán, also inhabited this city. The city's crest shows two lions ready to pounce, their paws clutching onto a golden tree covered in green foliage, on an azure field; it is bordered by a tressure (an ornamental fringe) charged with seven saltires gules on a field of gold; (a piece of armor which covers the head and face) with the visor closed, and the emblem (a motto beneath the crest), is a red banner charged with the cross potent on a lance and lambrequin (a feathery adornment). According to heraldry (the study of blazonry), the meaning of the Guadalajara's coat of arms is the following: the lions signify the esprit de corps; the tree, perseverance; the saltires gules, victory; the lances, strength and wisdom; the cross potent, the defense and practice of Christianity; and the helm argent, triumph in battle. During the war for independence, there were fewer than thirty-five thousand people living in the city. It was during that time that they cut off the supply line coming from Mexico City, which favored an opening for external commerce. Conflicts and historical events taking place in Guadalajara helped to forge the nation's destiny. In 1958, Benito Juárez was nearly assassinated. In 1860, it was the scene of ferocious battles between Liberals and Conservatives. During the time of the Revolution, war was constantly being waged in its plazas. Despite having been the stage for innumerable battles, Guadalajara's churches, convents and historical monuments remain nearly completely intact. The cathedral has three doorways created in the 16th Century. In the main entrance, there are three niches depicting St. Peter, St. Paul and the Ascension; it contains a circular gable in whose tympanum the Apostles witness the Assumption of Mary into Heaven.

The information that interested me most was left till the end. I couldn't continue to read: I felt dizzy. The bus was ready to leave. I sat down without showing my ticket. The bus driver was talking to a woman who was standing to the side of the door. She wore a black skirt and her legs were long. Her lips were bright red. The bus slowly pulled away. The driver continued his conversation with the same girl who had now made herself comfortable in the front seat. She stretched out her skirt and fixed her blouse, tight around her shapely figure.

The information on the poster allowed me to see the city with a strange sort of familiarity. I wanted to ask the bus driver if we were going to pass by the cathedral. But I didn't dare. The conversation with the woman in the black skirt was now in hushed tones. When had it grown dark? Night had risen over the asphalt, and I hadn't noticed.

In the airport, I didn't know what direction to take. Without my having any time to react, an airport employee approached me solicitously to assist me. I kindly turned him away, but he insisted on carrying my suitcase. I told him that I didn't have any money.

"Whatever you can give me is fine."

He put me in a line. I stuck my hand in my purse and took out the last five pesos that I had. I handed them to him knowing that it was the last bit of money I had. But, instead of a cordial "thank you," what I received was a look of disgust. He practically threw the money back at my feet. He looked at me with such scorn that he hit himself on the forehead and began to insult me in front of everybody. I couldn't believe what I was hearing. He pointed his finger at me. Everyone turned to stare at me. I felt an unfamiliar fright. I had never felt like that before: belittled, humiliated. I didn't know what to say or how to react. I wanted to be in another time, in another place, in another country. I began to whisper a prayer: *Let me love Thee, my Lord and my God, and see myself as I really am: a pilgrim in this world, a Christ-*

ian called to respect and love all whose lives I touch, those in authority over me or those under my authority, my friends and my enemies. Help me to conquer anger with gentleness, greed by generosity, apathy by fervor . . .

My prayers did not have the desired effect. The insults continued. I wanted to flee, but I just stood there. An airport security guard arrived to see what was going on.

"This nutcase just stiffed me," he said without further explanation. He turned around and pointed his finger at me until he reached the door and walked out. People looked at me suspiciously. They talked amongst themselves. I stopped myself from crying. I looked for a seat on the other side of the airport lobby. I needed to get away from the shame. I was feigning a serenity that I didn't feel. I was afraid that the same man was going to appear at any moment and drown me in an ocean of insults. I overcame my desire to run away with the return of an oppressive hunger. I remembered that I had not eaten since the night before.

It must have been divine intervention that caused me to do what I did next. With my boarding pass in hand, I went up to the place where they sold tacos and nachos. With the same tranquility that I felt every Sunday during Mass at the time of the offertory, I asked for two orders of nachos. The yellow cheese fell slowly and quivered over the freshly made tortilla chips. A bunch of jalapeño peppers fell in a disordered heap over the nachos. I slowly began to eat. The stress and anxiety had disappeared. Pope Clement's prayers had done the trick. I felt immune to any danger. When I finished with the first order of nachos, a girl with big, gray eyes gave me the second order in a paper bag. Calmly, I said, "I'll have to pay you back later because I don't have any money."

"Police! Police!" was her response.

I wasn't able to run away. With his pistol in hand, a policeman approached. "What's going on over here?" he said angrily.

It was as if someone had nailed my feet to the floor. I made no attempt to get away.

"This young lady," she said, pointing at me, "wants to get off without paying."

"Is that so?" asked the policeman, a little more at ease as he put his pistol away. Upon seeing his weapon in its holster, I felt like laughing and crying at the same time. "Why don't you want to pay?" he asked in a hoarse voice.

"No. I didn't say that I wasn't going to pay. I simply don't have any money at this exact moment, but my cousin is on her way, and she's bringing me the money."

The grace of God had put the words in my mouth. Nothing could happen to me. I remembered the prayer for times of danger: *Whosoever honors the Lord, He will show him the way.*

"Okay, we'll wait for her here," the policeman proclaimed.

I give Thee thanks, Oh, Lord, for Thou hath answered my prayer, showing me the way. . . . God wasn't going to permit me to miss my plane over an order of nachos. I couldn't imagine myself in jail or sweeping up the floors of the airport. With the poise that comes with faith, I asked the policeman, "Sir, may I at least sit down, please?"

"Sit," he replied, annoyed.

"*En el cielo una hermosa mañana . . . La guadalupana, la guadalupana, la guadalupana bajó al Tepeyac,*" I started to sing quietly the song to the Virgin of Guadalupe, patron saint of Mexico's poor.

The policeman smiled openly upon hearing me. He looked at me half-curious, half-surprised. "*Un indio llamado Juan Diego.*" I sang and ate at the same time. The policeman, amused, never stopped observing me. The minutes went by slowly. Suddenly, I heard my boarding call from the other side of the airport lobby. I waited for my sign to give the policeman the slip. After the second boarding call for my flight, Divine Providence, the same that had forsaken Jalpa, revealed itself in Guadalajara. In front of us appeared a blind man begging for money. "Spare some change for a poor blind man?"

Two individuals approached him: one took him by the arm as the other one emptied his pockets. When the police officer saw this, he became indignant, and with weapon in hand, he came to the blind man's assistance.

Show me the way . . . I ran as fast as I could, and in a matter of minutes, I had crossed the airport lobby and found myself in front of the man who collected the boarding passes for my flight. I was one of the last people to board the plane. I made myself comfortable in my seat. I fastened my seatbelt. I took a deep breath. My seat was next to the window. The wings of the airplane appeared huge to me. Like two needles, my eyes were pinned to them. It started to rain, and the wings were soaked. The plane took off without any difficulty. Could this be how the journey to heaven feels? The man sitting next to me smiled; his teeth shined like polished silver. I pressed my hands together, one against the other. My palms were sweaty. The stranger's voice sounded tender and mild.

"Going to Los Angeles?"

"Yes. To Los Angeles," I answered.

I concentrated on the rows of houses that began to appear beneath those wings of steel. Jalpa had stayed far behind. I could still distinguish the buildings in Guadalajara, and at that altitude, the buildings looked naked without walls or roofs. We passed over many fields; to me, they were dead sterile fields that couldn't provide for those of us who were hungry.

I had never traveled in an airplane before. It was a strange sensation. I checked my watch. It was eight o'clock at night. It was the time when we would gather in the parish rectory of the Church of Our Lord in Jalpa. The smell of food stirred me from my ruminations. I turned around, and a stewardess was serving a tray with a sandwich, something to drink, and some peanuts to the man who traveled next to me. I remembered that I had no money. I had already lied in the airport; I wasn't about to do the same thing on the plane. They might not let me go if I owed them money. That food must cost a lot of money, much more than the two orders of nachos that I had stolen in the airport. That deed began to wear on my conscience. I had never taken anything that didn't belong to me. Hunger made me do it. The aroma from the food tortured me. I tried to distract myself by singing a song: *I don't know what's on your lips, I don't know what's in your eyes, that takes control of my whimsy and makes my heart go crazy . . . At night . . .*

The plane suddenly shook. The stewardesses rushed to collect the trays. They all took their seats in back. The wings vibrated as if they were transistors. The smile on the face of the man next to me had turned into a terrified grimace. The airplane began to move from side to side as if it were a ball in the hands of two giants. A prayer to St. Jude Thaddeus was urgently needed: *Most Holy Apostle, St. Jude Thaddeus, faithful servant and friend of Jesus, the name of the traitor who delivered your beloved Master into the hands of His enemies has caused you to be forgotten by many. But the Church honors you, and I invoke you as the special advocate of those who are in trouble and in despair. I implore you to pray on this miserable child's behalf; you were granted the power to come to the rescue of those who have lost almost all hope. Help me to realize that through our faith we triumph over life's difficulties by the power of Jesus who loved us and gave His life for us. Come to my assistance that I may receive the consolation and succor of Heaven in all my needs, trials, and sufferings, particularly in this moment of danger when this plane is about to go down. Help me to reach Los Angeles safely and don't allow for the sacrifices of my mom and my aunt and my grandfather to have been in vain. . . And I promise, dear St. Jude, always to remember this tremendous blessing and . . .*

"Is it a storm?" It was the man sitting next to me who asked out loud.

No one answered. I continued to pray before impending death. I went from St. Jude to La Magnífica: "*My soul glorifies the Lord and my spirit rejoices in God my Savior. . .*" I couldn't continue with my prayer. I had to go to the bathroom. A strange glow emerged from the darkness and enveloped the plane.

"Get back in your seat!" The shout came, deep and sullen, from the back of the plane.

I continued to move forward. Many people had covered their heads with pillows; cries and screams came from every direction. I grabbed onto the seats in order to keep moving forward. I pushed open a small door. I had never seen such a little lavatory before. The lights went out. When I awoke, I was occupying two seats. A stewardess offered me something to drink. My hands trembled slightly. I smelled of alcohol. I had fainted in the bathroom. The sky had cleared up. We still had another hour left before we landed. Another stewardess came up to me with a blanket. I stayed there, my eyes fixed on the pilots' cabin. Was it real or was I imagining it? The same strange glow that had enveloped the airplane now came out of the cockpit. I invoked La Magnífica once again: *He has performed mighty deeds with His arm; He has scattered those who are proud in their innermost thoughts. He has brought down rulers from their thrones but has lifted up the humble.* The light covered my face. I closed my eyes. An indescribable peace enveloped me, and I didn't feel frightened again for the rest of the trip.

A dull thud on the pavement and a light screeching of the tires indicated that we had landed. Some of the passengers applauded. I got off the plane. I wasn't afraid. My fears were left back in Jalpa. We formed two lines to present our documentation to the immigration officials. I looked for an exit. I had already done it once; I could take off running again like I did at the airport in Mexico. Once in the street, it would be very difficult for them to catch me.

There were officers with dogs at the exits. The security was tight. The line moved forward, and my ideas for slipping by the security weren't coming so easily. There were two officers: a dark-skinned woman and a man who was about sixty years old. The woman was delayed with the interrogation of an entire family. There was no other way out. Three more people, and then it was my turn. The stress tied knots in my spine. I had to go up to the man who, now seen at a shorter distance, looked younger than before. I handed him my passport. His thin lips drew tight with an air of displeasure. He looked at me; his eyes were two deep fathoms crowned by a pair of bushy, black eyebrows. He had a wrinkled forehead and an abundance of mostly white hair. I handed him my passport and my pulse quickened . . . *Help me to make it through this predicament. Cloud his vision so that he doesn't see that it's expired . . . Don't let them send me back . . . Touch his heart of stone . . .*

"Another I.D.!" He made me tremble with his shout.

With the courage of knowing that Divine Providence was with me, I replied, with a smile, "That's all I have."

"What are you doing in Los Angeles?"

"I'm on a two-week vacation," I responded calmly.

"How much money do you have?"

. . . Christ resurrected, enlighten me . . . Guide me, Holy Spirit . . . "A thousand dollars," I said firmly.

"Show it to me," he ordered, flexing his arms.

. . . *My Lord, my God, I place my faith in Thee* . . . I started to shake. . . . *Lead me as You led Andrew and his brother Peter* . . . "Don't you trust me?" The words came out smoothly. "Because I was taught not to show money out in public. What if someone robs me? Then what would I do?" *May Your strength protect me* . . .

"Okay," he said annoyed. He wrote on a piece of paper. "You have a permit for fifteen days." He stamped my expired passport . . . *Blessed be God, forever!*

The path to retrieve my luggage seemed very long to me. It was like walking through a tunnel and coming out into the light. It was still September 16th. The parade in Jalpa was now far behind. I began to forget about it. My aunt came to greet me. I wrapped my arms around her neck. She hurried me toward the airport exit: "There's no more danger once we're outside."

We walked to the parking lot. All I thought about was the hot meal that awaited me.

Teresa
Los Angeles, California

I Saw How They Raped Her

They had just fired me, and I couldn't believe it. Ten years of working for La Primorosa, a textile factory where they told me, "We don't need you anymore."

My humanity was reduced to a mere object that could be cast aside with no more consideration than a supervisor's whim. I lived in Colombia, a country of 36 million inhabitants, a nation with vast natural resources, but known for its violence and narcotrafficking.

Though I had a girlfriend, marriage could wait for a few more years. I ventured to start up my own business with the money that they gave me from the factory when I was laid off. I opened up a bicycle shop that soon prospered. Being my own boss gave me a lot of joy. I woke up very early each morning and closed shop very late each night. That was the road to prosperity. My income was growing and I started to save money.

The news that arrived at my business made me happy. The government was dealing serious blows to the mafia. The cartels were falling apart. Justice was beginning to prevail. Everyone desired peace.

It was six o'clock in the morning when I saw the letter among some misplaced boxes of parts. It didn't have a postal mark or a return address. Someone must have shoved it through a crack overnight. I peeked out onto the sidewalk. At that time of the morning, the street was practically deserted.

I hesitated to open the letter. Fear had been unleashed inside of me. How could I receive such a letter? I guessed at its contents. Some of my friends had already received them. But why me? I wasn't rich, just a bicycle shop owner. I tore open the envelope.

> Henry,
>
> Beginning Friday of next month, we will pass by your shop to collect a monthly fee of 5,000 pesos. The money must be all there. It's a small price to pay if you compare it to the value of your life and the lives of your family. We know who they are, where they live, and the places they go. Don't even think about reporting this to the police. If you do, you can kiss your stinking life good-bye. We're experts at tying neckties, and we send them gift-wrapped.

Neckties had become famous in Colombia. They would kidnap the person who refused to pay; and if he were male, they would cut off his penis and attach it to his own neck. That's how his family would find him. This sort of extortion was so common that people referred to it as a "vaccination." I couldn't believe that people like that actually existed. But they did. The newspapers gave accounts of their deeds. Everyone knew that it was some kind of octopus-type organization. Its deadly tentacles had already touched many lives.

I took off all my clothes. I stepped into the bathtub. The steam from the water had fogged up the mirrors. I was terrified at the idea that someone could come and kill me. I imagined myself in the newspapers, naked, stabbed in the back. My bloody corpse wrapped in sheets. They had killed an entire family like that. They had put them in a bathtub, one on top of the other, the parents, two brothers, and a nephew. A circle of red blood on the floor.

FAMILY KILLED FOR REFUSING "VACCINATION"

Five members of the same family were found dead in an area around Bogotá. The manner in which they were stabbed and the circumstances surrounding their death give reason to believe that they are the most recent victims of a group of gangsters who have dedicated themselves to terrorizing all of Bogotá with their so-called "vaccinations."

"They told us the week before that they weren't going to give a penny to the people who were trying to extort money from them," stated Vincent Magnum, brother-in-law to one of the victims.

The newspapers also reported that the authorities had declared themselves impotent against this gang. I waited until after dinner. It was obvious that something was bothering me. I hadn't been able to eat a bite. I bit my lower lip. How could I break the news to them? How could I tell them that I would have to leave the country as a result of my honest work? How could I explain to them that in thirty days I could be stabbed to death? I needed the strength to tell them about it.

The door opened. My father had just gotten back from work.

"They're going to kill me," I said, without beating around the bush.

"Who would want to kill you?" my mother asked incredulously.

I showed them the letter. My father read it out loud. My mother's face went pale. I rushed to hold her and help her sit down in a chair.

"Why you?" she asked as her voice trembled.

I gave her a kiss on the forehead. When I heard her sobbing, I couldn't hold back the tears. In the end, we agreed that the best thing for me to do was to leave the country.

I had a strange dream that night. Two men came into my room. They tied me up from the neck down to my feet. I wanted to wake up, but I couldn't. My body took a beating on the bumpy road. They stopped in front of a cliff. Drops of blood ran from the sheet. I woke up as I fell into the abyss.

The following day, I went to work as if nothing had happened. It was important not to raise any suspicions. It was very likely that they were watching me. On the way to work, a policeman pulled me over. He accused me of running a stop sign. I burst out laughing. The law was enforcing stop signs while a band of professional killers terrorized the city. Disconcerted, the policeman removed his cap covered with insignias. His hair was gray. My laughter became intertwined with a wail erupting from deep within. He looked at me, but I couldn't stop laughing and wailing at the same time. He closed his infractions booklet. And he let me go.

On Friday of that same week, I presented my case before the United States Consulate. My life was in danger. They couldn't deny me a visa. Irritated, the immigration officer replied in broken Spanish, "How do we know that you didn't write this letter?"

An electrifying rage coursed through my body. I wanted to hit him. The muscles at the back of my neck stiffened. Composing myself, I disputed the decision. I asked him to consider my situation. I didn't want to leave. I was being forced to do so.

"This letter, *tú inventar*. Anyways, there is no political asylum in the *Estadous Unidous* for you people."

I left, infuriated. There were twenty-one days left before my time was up. A week went by. My parents helped me calm down. Somehow I had to escape. I came to the point of contemplating staying there and confronting death. Perhaps it was my destiny to die this way. The advertisement was on a large panel; It took up a quarter of the page: "Excursions to Central America and the United States." I cut out the announcement.

That afternoon, I went home earlier than usual. I opened the door and there was my girlfriend. I hadn't gone by to see her in two weeks. Her eyes were swollen. My mother had told her everything. We went for a walk. My temples were pounding. How could I tell her that I wasn't sure if we would ever get married, that all of the plans that we made had come to an end? She was tall and beautiful. We stopped at the corner. We hid behind a lush tree. I pulled her close to me. I caressed her face. She wrapped her arms around my neck. I kissed her forehead, her nose, and her lips. She put my hand on her heart. It beat rapidly. I promised to write to her every day.

My departure was scheduled for a Friday at five o'clock in the morning. I said good-bye to my parents in a whisper. No one could find out that I was leaving. When I closed the door, I could hear my mother sobbing. I was filled with rage upon leaving my home. I walked with closed fists. Why did I have to leave my country against my will? I wanted to put the heads of those who had forced me to do this in a guillotine.

There were twenty-five Colombians on the "excursion." The plan was to get to the United States, where some friends would pay for my relocation. I was surprised to notice three young girls in the group. The plan consisted of passing ourselves off as tourists: we would visit various cities, and upon our arrival in Mexico, we would be turned over to the hands of some "coyotes."

"Those coyotes are sacks of shit," said one of the travelers.

In San Andrés Island, the sky was a shade of indigo, and in Tegucigalpa, we were met with a downpour. They took us to a modest, but clean, hotel. I spent that night admiring the bright stars. We flew to San Salvador, and with little rest, we went on to Guatemala. I nearly fainted there. The hotel rooms where they took us were real pigsties. I needed to rest; my temples were throbbing.

"Wake up, motherfucker! And give me what you got!"

Was I dreaming?

"Hurry up before I kick your ass!"

Two hooded men, armed. They were ordering me to give them all of my belongings. I wasn't able to react. One of them yanked me by the sleeve and threw me to the ground. His voice was authorative.

"Hurry up before we lose our patience!"

As a precaution, I had split up my money and put it in different places. I had the majority of it sown into my underwear. I took my backpack out from under the bed. They snatched it away from me, rummaged through it, and found two $10 bills. They threw my backpack on the bed and ran out of the room. I allowed a few minutes to go by. I opened the door, and in the hallway, I saw how the young girls embraced each other, frightened. They had been robbed as well. I encouraged them to report it to the hotel manager. When we arrived, the others were already giving notice of the robbery. They had robbed everyone else, too. A tall, bony man, with an elongated profile, dark skin, big teeth, and very pronounced, fat lips denied having seen anything. The name of the hotel was The Viceroy; we badmouthed it as we left, calling it "The Po' Boy."

We boarded a bus that took us on another "tour." Bunches of men and women got on at every stop: women stepped on with children wrapped up in their *rebozos*; men with blackened fingernails clutched their bundles of vegetables. A short, well-dressed old man got on with a rooster that had golden feathers. The bus was filled to the brim. The sun passed through the windows and covered our faces like balsam. The drive lasted ten hours. Guatemala was not as small as I thought.

A soldier motioned for us to stop. The bus driver suddenly hit the brakes. An authoritative voice could be heard: "All of the men step off!" Disconcerted, we obeyed.

The group of soldiers surrounded the bus. One by one we got off the bus. A soldier with dark skin, a round face, and stout arms and legs, ordered us, "Put your hands on your head!"

I was late to react. A kick to the groin made me yell. I fell to my knees. I wasn't the only one they knocked around.

"Everybody keep your hands up!"

They searched our chests, our waists, and even squeezed our genitals.

"They don't have anything! We've already checked them up the ass!" said the dark-skinned guy who had struck me.

"Check their passports!" the authoritative voice of their commander could be heard again.

The soldier who checked my passport came up to my ear and said, "You're not bringing any cocaine from Colombia, are you, wetback?"

All that registered with me was: "Colombia," "cocaine." The word "wetback" was new for me.

"You guys are going up north, right?"

"Yes, sir," I said defiantly. I expected another beating. The soldier walked away.

Our "tour guide" tried to calm us down. He directed himself to the one who was giving the orders, a man with a plain complexion who bit his fist. They took a number of steps back. It was a private meeting. After about twenty minutes, and after exchanging "greetings," the "guides" returned. "Everyone on the bus!" they ordered.

It was completely silent on the bus. One of the youngest guys traveling with us was bleeding from his bottom lip. We reached the border with Mexico. Mexican hospitality was famous in Colombia.

"Fucking *pinches* Colombians . . . Stand over there, you

fucking bastards, *hijos de la chingada*. We're going to check you up the ass to make sure you're not bringing any cocaine."

It was the first time that I had ever heard the words: "*pinches*" and "*chingada*." One by one, we were taken to a room, including the women and children. It was a small space; there was a table and a chair in the middle; and a light bulb hung from a beam in the ceiling. They ordered me to take off my clothes. They inspected them thoroughly. They took my backpack somewhere else, and when I got it back, it was missing half of its contents. Another private conversation ensued among the "guides" before they let us go. They escorted us "tourists" to another bus that was already waiting for us. The soldiers continued to check the other passengers.

The bus driver was very young; he must have only been about nineteen years old. His bright eyes looked us up and down. His cheekbones jutted out, his nose was flat. I said hello. He did not reply. Along the way, I observed the other passengers that were on his bus. Just looking at them, you could see how humble they were: the majority were barefoot, their feet flat, broken in. I watched as a woman with curly hair suckled her child. When she realized that I was observing her, she lifted her *rebozo* up to her shoulder.

The journey was long and exhausting. There was only one stop to eat and instead of eating, most of us ran to the bathroom. The fright had loosened our bowels. We resumed the voyage; and after many long hours, we stopped in front of a very nice hotel—the best on the entire trip. We stayed there for a whole day and night. One of the coyotes told us to leave our backpacks, and they would return them to us later at the airport. One of the Central Americans who came on the bus, told us, "That's a big, fat lie. What they really want is to take your best stuff."

I removed my shirts and pants from my backpack. I put on everything, one on top of the other. All I left inside were my dirty clothes.

They took us to the airport very early in the morning. For the first time, I noticed how noisy the bus was. It seemed as if it was going to fall apart on the road. We almost missed our flight to Tijuana because the traffic was so slow. Arriving in such a hurry helped us to avoid responding to any questions. We boarded the airplane to Tijuana as a group of tourists, and we said good-bye to our guides.

The plane's elevation created a buzz in my temples. I was tired and bewildered. I closed my eyes. I hadn't slept well in days. It was nighttime when we landed in Tijuana. A bone-chilling cold accompanied us to the house where we stayed the night.

There were five people waiting in the house. There weren't enough beds, so we made ourselves comfortable on the floor. The three girls who came on the trip looked exhausted; they had dark circles around their eyes. All three looked alike. They must have been sisters: the big, bright eyes, the blonde hair, the fair skin. One of them had an upturned nose full of freckles. I hadn't once heard them complain. They talked amongst themselves. The one who appeared to be the youngest had a mole over her right cheekbone. She never left the others' sides. Where were those Colombian girls going? Had they also received a "vaccination" threat, and now they were fleeing like me? I imagined them at a dance: boisterous, smiling, refusing those who approached them to dance. Flirtatious, donning new dresses that showed their naked arms.

There were no problems crossing. We rode in a van. With everyone stacked on top of each other, the drive was torturous. I couldn't breathe. My legs started to go numb. The van stopped in front of a two-story house. It seemed to be abandoned.

"We made it across! Get down!" The fat guide took the lead.

“Hurry them up, Güero . . .”

“Hey, are we in the Unites States yet?” asked somebody.

“Yes,” answered El Güero unwillingly.

For the first time, I noticed why they called him El Güero: the whiteness of his skin, his chestnut hair, his beady eyes and cold expression. We hadn’t gone far from the border. The border fence could still be seen.

“C’mon, hurry up and get in here! What’re you waiting for?” said El Güero.

We piled up in front of the door. The fat guy had opened it wide. The stench that came from the house penetrated my nose. It smelled like human excrement. The girls covered their mouths and noses with the hollow of their hands. One of them screamed when she spotted a rat coming from a mattress laid in the middle of the room. There were bars on the windows; and in the backyard, there was a large patio full of the skeletons of trees. Some rusty, old swings rested motionless over a pile of dead leaves.

The guides argued amongst themselves: “Hey, fucker, so are we going to jump the job, or what?” El Güero stared pensively at the floor.

The other one insisted, “I need to unload.”

El Güero replied, “All right, let’s jump them.”

The fat guy showed his big, yellow teeth. He scratched his bulbous head, and then stroked his beard showing the growth from various days. He insisted that we sit on the floor. He ordered the girls from Colombia to sit next to the door. No one objected. We stayed like that for a very long time.

The sun was bright, but we were shivering with cold. The fat guy appeared in the doorway; he never took his eyes off of the youngest of the girls from Colombia. She clung onto the one who seemed to be the oldest.

“Everybody up to stretch your legs! Walk down to the end of the hallway!”

It was hard for us to walk. The hallway was dark. We barely fit. We moved forward slowly, holding onto the wall. A door opened in front of us. The light illuminated the hallway. There was a fence around the backyard patio.

"Anyone who looks over that fence is fucked." The warning came from the fat guy.

We hurried out. We ventured to walk up to the end of the property. It was an almost deserted area. Very nearby could be seen the straight, recently brushed back mountains that separated us from Mexico.

The sun and the fresh air that bathed our faces made us all feel better. We joked. For a moment, we actually felt like tourists.

I had to go to the bathroom so I went to the back room. I didn't see the girls anywhere. I ventured down the long hallway. At the end of the hallway, there was a small set of stairs where strange noises could be heard. I went to investigate. An icy chill sent a shiver down my spine. My knees were shaking. I went upstairs without making a sound. A solitary light escaped through a crack in the door of the first room. I got closer. I pushed the open door softly. This could not be happening. How can I describe what I was seeing?

"Pigs! Murderers! What have you done?"

The three sisters, who had not been separated during the entire trip, the ones who protected each other, the ones who laughed quietly, were being raped. The oldest one, naked, face up on the bed, with her open eyes, moaned softly. The sheet between her legs was soaked with blood. I thought my temples were going to explode. A pair of eyes looked at me, pleading. They called out for help. It was the youngest one, the one with the dark mole on her right cheek. She was on the floor on all fours, with her clothes all torn up. There she was, the girl from Colombia. One of the Mexicans was holding her by the hair with his penis inside of her mouth, as the other one held her by the waist, raping her from behind. Upon seeing me, they got up, furious: "What the fuck are you doing here?" With his fly open, holding up his pants that were falling down around his knees, the fat guy pulled out a gun. El Güero, springing to his feet, grabbed me. It felt like a thousand needles were being hammered into my temples. The blow was hard and precise. Blood gushed from my mouth and cheeks. Everything was blurry. Staggering, I tried to step back. I was spitting blood.

"Are we going to kill this fucker?"

"No . . . No. They still owe us a lot of money for him."

Another blow with the pistol, right between the eyes. The impact from the strike caused me to stagger onto the stairs. I fell back. I tumbled down, head over heels, until I hit the floor.

"Wow. This is a deep gash that they gave you," said the same short man with jutting cheekbones who had asked if we were in the United States yet.

"If we were in El Salvador, it would be over for those sons of bitches." He explained to me how I had lost consciousness when I fell. "You are one heavy man. We had to drag you. You'll end up with a big scar, that's all."

They all looked at me, horrified, as we waited for the rapists to appear. I still felt like I had a thousand needles hammered into my temples. I cursed all Mexicans. Several minutes transpired. No one dared to take a peek when the arrival of a car was heard. Without looking at anybody, El Güero rushed outside. He spoke in a low whisper at the door. Screeching tires could be heard as the car sped away.

The door opened. It was the other guide, who ordered us to make ourselves comfortable in a van that was bigger than the one before. His black eyes fixed on me: "You're coming up front with me."

It was the longest ride of the whole trip. I thought that

I'd never make it to Los Angeles alive. They had to make sure that we wouldn't turn them in. The coyote drove carefully; I watched him out of the corner of my eye. He handed me a baseball cap and a clean shirt. "Put this on." He bundled up my bloody shirt and hid it in a paper bag underneath the seat. He was older than the rest. Gray hair covered his temples. He spoke slowly, as if to choose his words carefully. "El Güero told me about the girls. That's why they're not here. They took them back to the other side so that they could bring them across separately."

You bunch of pigs! They could be dead.

"You don't believe me, do you?"

I kept quiet. I recalled the pleading look from the young girl who was being violated in the most brutal, most inhuman fashion.

"Are they dead?" The question surprised him.

He looked at me with suppressed rage. "Man, what kind of question is that? How could you think that they're dead? You'll see. You'll run into them somewhere around here when you least expect it."

I felt a profound disdain for that man who was also another accomplice to those rats.

The van pulled off the highway. It drove onto a dirt road full of thorns. It stopped in front of a house hidden behind a row of trees.

"Everybody down!" The order was to wait until the Border Patrol from San Clemente had left. We went ahead keeping to one side of the bushes. The thorns stuck us all over our bodies. The house had windows that were sealed from within. Each room had a door with a metal gate, simulating prison cells. I was paralyzed with fear. The two men who had struck me came out of one of the rooms. The taller one approached me. "If you say anything, you're fucked."

We stayed at that house for three days waiting for the

immigration from San Clemente to leave. They split us up into groups in the "cells." A piece of sweet bread and a soda pop was our daily meal. To go to the bathroom, we had to ask for permission, and one of the guides would open the gate that covered the door. The bathroom was in such a putrid state that using it made you want to puke. At dawn on the third day, we were taken out of our cells and escorted to a van that was closer to the door. The windows were covered with thick curtains. They warned us not to look out. We drove with some people sitting on top of others. This was our final journey. We could hear the voices of all three coyotes. Those vultures were laughing, but I couldn't stop thinking about the three sisters, the three friends, about the pleading look from the youngest one, the one with the dark mole on her right cheek.

The air wasn't circulating. We started to cough. I thought we were going to suffocate when the van stopped in front of a wooden house. We got out, one by one. Some were coughing; others covered their mouths. I was the last to get off the van. The fat guy and El Güero wouldn't stop staring at me. I thought they were going to get rid of me. No one would ever find me in that large, quasi-abandoned house.

"They owe us a lot of money for him," one of them said.

They ordered me to call my friends, and charged them more than what had been previously agreed.

Henry
Downey, California

The Killings Were Commonplace

The phone rang just before dawn. I picked up the receiver, certain that it was bad news. Bad news always come just before dawn. I walked to the kitchen. The sun would be coming up soon. It was cloudy, and the wind rattled the only window that looked to the outside of the house. I wanted to open it and scream out into the street that they had just murdered my father in El Salvador, but it was jammed. There's no need for a motive to kill someone in El Salvador. The corpses of barefoot men, with dark skin, swollen lips, and the signs of torture on their bodies appeared in the morning, on the sidewalks, on high mountain tops, in the fields of corn.

Like my father, I grew up in El Salvador, land of volcanoes, of open craters, of coffee plantations that spread across the mountainsides like lava. And just like my father, I delighted in the ecstasy of fragrances from *ayates*, avocados, elder berries, guayabas, papayas, and maguey.

To live in El Salvador is to drink instant coffee in the country that ranks third in world coffee production. It is to live in a land of plains and valleys where heavy rains are followed by severe droughts.

My father lay dead in El Salvador as I stood staring out my window in Los Angeles. A couple with their arms around each other walked across the street, eluding the cars. My father had told me over and over again that I should get out of

El Salvador. I never wanted to do it until the killing started.

I hadn't wanted to hear the details of his death. My mother tearfully warned me not to talk to anyone: "Things are getting worse, son. Make sure no one finds out that you're coming back." I promised her I would leave right away.

I boarded the plane carrying only my birth certificate. I had returned as part of history. A history of exodus, of fear, of repression for not belonging to a particular group. A history filled with protagonists and deserters. El Salvador riddled itself with bullets. The war, the filth, the helplessness. The slain bodies of university classmates, the flight to the United States, all stirred in my sleeping recollections. It had been six months since I had last written to my girlfriend. Would she still remember me?

Hail-sized rain accompanied me to my parents' house. I would have never emigrated to the United States if it had not been for the incident. I was very close to finishing my degree at the National University of El Salvador. I felt fortunate; I had parents who supported me, brothers and sister, and my university studies.

El Salvador had a new president, Colonel Arturo Armando Molina. The government pointed to the National University of El Salvador as a safe haven for government opposition.

On July 19, 1972, the sun rose just as it had on July 18. The mountains with their green skirts sprinkled with clusters of coffee. The soda pop, orange, and corn-on-the-cob vendors near the sidewalk of the university. Young men looking at young women through the windows. It was sunny on the university campus, and the girls laughed, some whispered, out on the patio. Others walked hastily to their classes. It all started like an earthquake: the windows, the doors, and even the walls shook before those gigantic machines making way. They were tanks that, like dragons, spewed fire through their elongated orifices. We dropped down to the floor. The girls who were whispering out on the patio had disappeared. As if they had come out of the green mountains, war planes spit out bullets that lodged in the walls of the university. Professors shouted frantically for us to get down on the ground. The soldiers got out of their tanks and advanced along the corridor. My arrhythmia made it difficult for me to breathe. The door to the administration gave way to rifle butts, and the rector of the university was arrested along with the director of the school of medicine. The buzzing of the bullets had stopped, and students began to flee. They caught many of the students; almost a thousand were arrested. From that day forward, my life would not be the same. The hope for change in El Salvador had died. My father implored me: "Go. Things are only going to get worse. Nothing's going to happen to us older folks. The danger is with the children and the young people."

I obeyed. I said good-bye to him, making him promise that they would follow after me. Even though he said yes, I knew that he wasn't going to do it. El Salvador was his country, the cornfields his joy, the volcanoes his sanctuary. On the way to the United States embassy, I decided that I would go to Miami. A lot of rich people from El Salvador lived there.

El Salvador is a very small country, tiny, teeny tiny, but with huge differences in incomes and lifestyles. The wealthy families—the fourteen mentioned in *Time Magazine*, but really there aren't just fourteen, rather there are hundreds, because one has to take into account their cousins, their children, their grandchildren, their sons-in-law, their daughters-in-law—those families, known to everyone as the proprietors of the nation, have a house in the capital, another in Miami, and a country estate close to their farms. The suffering of the farm workers can be seen all around their homes. They can almost touch it, but they dare not; the poor, or the "chusma" as they refer to them, are practically invisible. They drive along the boulevards in their Mercedes, their Jaguars. The rich of El Salvador always have their sights set high, delighting in the volcano landscapes. The poor keep their eyes to the ground, looking at the craters in the mountains like open wounds.

I was able to acquire a visa without any difficulty, and I had a pleasant flight to Miami. Arriving in Miami was like going to a city in Latin America. Spanish was spoken everywhere; the streets were clean and well designed; there weren't any boys with uneven humps begging for money in the civic center, nor were there any starving women with their children tied to their backs selling fruit.

Miami was definitely an ideal city for me. All I needed to do was find a job, go to school, and then I could work on one of those great, big, luxurious cruise liners that comes with a swimming pool and gym for its occupants. I thought that in a few years I would have saved up enough money to return to El Salvador and invite my whole family to eat breakfast at the Sheraton in San Salvador. That is where all of the well-to-do families go to play golf, drink whiskey, and admire the volcanoes.

They didn't let me go to school in Miami because I only had a tourist visa, and with the job that I got as a dishwasher, I wasn't going to make enough money for my plans. I decided to move to Los Angeles, where I discovered that there were a lot of Salvadorans. They had converted a section of the city into a smaller version of Central America. I relished in eating *pupusas* (corn tortillas filled with beans).

The airport in El Salvador was situated on the outskirts of the city. To get to the city, one must drive along a lonely road. Two years had transpired since I had passed along that same road in order to leave the country, and now I was going back. For the outside world, my father was just a statistic, one of the ten people killed each day in El Salvador. "Conflicts between the left and the right wings," the newspapers in the United States would report.

We buried him in a cemetery a short distance from our home. We weren't the only ones: there were many graves ready to receive their coffins. The cries, laments, and dismay could be seen around every tomb. As we left the cemetery, more coffins, followed by their mourners, continued to arrive. The cemeteries had become the most frequented places in the city. It was said that the streets of El Salvador had been turned into death traps. In whispers, people commented about the kidnappings, mass murders, and the washed blood that ran along the sidewalks. My mother and my brothers cried silently in stoic resignation; they agreed not to inquire about what had happened.

The second good-bye is always harder than the first because you don't want to leave. The aroma pulls you to your roots, to the fields and to the cities. In the end, I convinced myself that it was for the best. There was the smell of gunpowder in the air and a large-scale war was on its way. This time I didn't go back alone: my mother asked me to take my sister with me. I agreed without considering the risk.

I promised my girlfriend that I would return soon so that we could get married. She had greeted me as if no time had transpired between us. She was sure that I would be back. I held her tightly and kissed her on the lips.

There is an area in El Salvador where the "gringos" live. They can be seen at the market on Sundays wearing sandals and T-shirts; but during the week, they're always well-dressed. Many of them are associates of *The Families*; others are extended family members. There are also those who make their living by crossing people into the United States. We found a successful Mexican-American who dedicated himself to that sort of business. We agreed upon the conditions of our departure. The Mexican embassy gave us tourist visas, and we went on our way to Mexico with the plan to cross into the United States.

We left El Salvador remembering the dead; there were more and more each day. They woke up with their mouths singed, their hands amputated.

An orange-colored sun, just beginning to appear over the volcanoes, accompanied us for a long stretch of the way. The Mexican-American spoke little; his rough, dry voice provided us with information about the cities that we would visit in Mexico. A good portion of the journey would be traveled by car. His countenance went unchanged when some police vehicle would drive up next to him. His status as a foreigner gave him confidence. He wasn't afraid of anyone coming to his door at night. He was a businessman, protected by the law.

On our first stop for gas, I took advantage of his distraction to jot down the car's license plate number, and carefully, I opened the glove compartment and took a look at his documentation. I copied down his driver's license and his address in Los Angeles.

We traveled for many hours. We stopped at two hotels before reaching the city that impressed me the most in Mexico: Puerto Vallarta. The exuberance of the landscape momentarily caused me to forget about the dead. It lifted the fear that I felt while on the road. I couldn't fathom such colonial beauty. It was a paradise where there was no war, no hunger, though I realized later that poverty did exist. We stayed there for a few days. I liked the sound that the rocks made when I walked across them. My sister was amused by my admiration.

"You're like a little child."

"Look! What a beautiful restaurant."

"Come on. Let's go to that restaurant then. I don't know about you, but I'm hungry."

We passed by the restaurants and admired the houses of the stars.

"You can go over to Elizabeth Taylor's house, and I'll go by Richard Burton's. What do you think?"

"You're still acting crazy. Go ahead then. You go in first and I'll follow you."

We ran through the cobblestone streets like children until we stood before a large gate that opened up to the Burtons' famous residence. A chambermaid asked us if we had seen it yet. The thought that there were two houses, joined by a bridge, which had been inhabited by Elizabeth Taylor and Richard Burton, filled us with excitement.

"Come on. Let's go check them out," I said to my sister who followed me everywhere. *I wouldn't leave her alone for a second with the Mexican-American,* I thought to myself.

"No," she said. "What? Do you think we're on vacation? What if the man is looking for us?"

"Yeah. You're right. Let's go."

"No. Come on. Let's sit down here for a little while."

We sat on a corner of the sidewalk. Her round face, her big eyes, like two almonds, filled with tears. She was thinking about the dangers that were in store for our brothers in El Salvador.

That afternoon, the Mexican-American arrived with instructions for us to leave for Guadalajara that same evening. From there we would go to Tijuana. It didn't look anything like Puerto Vallarta. Our guide took us to a coyote's house. I learned along the way that that's what they called those who took undocumented people across the border.

"Oh, lord. He's been in prison for a while now," a lady with fat arms told our guide.

Without getting discouraged, our guide assured us that

he was well connected with other coyotes. He took us to a hotel that was more or less clean. He told us that we would be safe there, and that his "associate" would join us in a few hours. It was already very late. His "associate" never showed up. Nor did the Mexican-American.

"Hey, what if we look for a coyote on our own?" I asked my sister.

"You think he left us here hanging?" She replied in disbelief.

"Yeah." *That son of a bitch,* I thought but didn't say it out loud. "Come on." I took her by the hand. "You're just like our mother. A courageous woman. And we're so close to the United States already. If that dumbass really did leave us, then we'll have to find somebody to take us across. What do you say?"

"Whatever you decide is okay with me."

I pressed her against my chest. At that moment the door opened violently. For an instant, I thought I was in El Salvador, that I had dreamt up our visit to Puerto Vallarta and that before me were soldiers who had come to make me "disappear." I was scared with a capital "S." The police gave us orders that we couldn't understand. Frustrated, they went back to doublecheck the address. They had the wrong place.

"Well, that's okay. We'll just take these *pollos* in and see what we can get from them."

They took us to an office where we learned that they had confused us with some counterfeiters. They wanted to place each of us in a separate cell. I asked them to allow my sister to remain in the office. They ignored me. We were very surprised when we saw the Mexican-American who had taken us out of El Salvador. He looked very beaten up. Someone who appeared to be in charge took him out and left him in the office. He had blood on his eyebrows, on his lips, and on his shirt. On our first night there, we listened as they beat him again. I recalled those who had died in El Salvador once again. The pain of burying my father without inquiring about his murderers. Prison torture was not only committed in the dungeons of El Salvador but in Mexican jails as well. We endured four days of terror, shouts, moans, and harsh, rough, and sharp beatings. We were in a cell with twenty-two other detainees, some accused of petty crimes, others of rape, and the majority of theft.

On the third day, the Mexican-American was permitted to leave. He promised that he would obtain some more money to release us, but we never saw him again. Our nightmare came to an end on the fifth day. I left that place certain that all jails were exactly alike: torture chambers bearing signs alluding to honor and patriotism. There was a Mexican flag hanging above the desk where the one who appeared to be the captain sat. High on the wall, a plaque proclaimed: "Traffic and Police Department, serving the people of Baja California with honesty and efficacy."

We reached downtown Tijuana by taxi. We walked around looking for a coyote. We were approached by many of them. We selected one who turned out to be a nice person. He took us to his house. The authorities had taken away what money we had, and the Mexican-American never came back to help us.

"You guys want to eat?" the coyote asked us.

I looked at my sister.

"Yeah, I'm hungry."

The man hailed a taxi. "Get in," he said.

We went to a house nearby. We were so hungry we could have eaten a horse. The coyote told us that all he had was a few eggs for frying, and if we wanted *nopales*, we had to cut them ourselves.

"Hey, can you believe the Mexicans actually eat cactus?" observed my sister.

The hunger I felt was more painful than the piercing of the cactus needles. I cut off a few nopales, and I removed the needles with a knife. Without cooking them, I mixed them up with the eggs. It seemed like a succulent dish to us.

We left early in the morning on the following day, headed toward the line that separates Mexico from the United States. We were joined by another group that also wanted to go across. The coyote gave us instructions: "Change your names, and no matter what you do, don't say that you're from El Salvador."

We made up different names; I was going to say that we were from Michoacan and that we were coming from Puerto Vallarta.

We began to walk over a long trail; the rough crags made it difficult. The coyote was always at the head of the group to warn us of any dangers. After many hours, a helicopter, like a giant bird, illuminated our heads. We ran in every direction. Our hearts skipped another beat in our chests. It was once again June 26, the day after the general strike in El Salvador. Tanks and armed soldiers, immigration officers looking for us. Hundreds of armed soldiers firing into the buildings. Students lying down on the floor. The coyote and everyone else lying on the ground.

A soldier shouted, "Don't any of you move!"

An officer yelled at my girlfriend, "Don't you move!"

Sixteen students killed in El Salvador.

"Everybody out!" said the same authoritative voice.

We all came out with our hands up. There were no gunshots. No one had been killed. We provided false information, and they deported us to Tijuana.

My sister and I looked for the Mexican-American with whom we had initiated our journey from El Salvador. We had hoped to find him so that he could give us back some of the money that we had paid him.

"The Mexican-American is long gone," said the coyote.

"So he wouldn't have to pay the coyote?"

"Yes, so he wouldn't have to pay the coyote."

"You guys have already suffered a great deal. I'll get you across," said the coyote who had recently attempted to cross us.

We asked him to let us rest for a day, and that's what we did.

"Everything has been arranged. You guys are going to walk across together with this young man," he told us.

My legs were trembling, but I made it across; my sister summoned all of her courage and crossed as well. The young man resisted. He stepped forward, then went back again. My sister and I made signals for him to pass. He finally took a chance. Led by the coyote's assistant, we went directly to the airport. I ventured to buy the tickets. We calmly took our seats in order to wait for our plane. The young man got up to go to the bathroom. A few minutes later, a number of uniformed officers approached us and asked for our papers. "Oh, no, not again!"

They grabbed us by the arm and took us to the office, to be fingerprinted, interrogated, and then deported. With our experience from the first time, it was easier for us to pass for Mexicans. They deported us to a different part of Tijuana. We took a taxi and went to the coyote's house. He welcomed us warmly, saying, "I was starting to miss you already. Especially the Salvadoran rice that your sister makes."

"Was it the rice or my sister that you missed?" I asked him, laughing.

Very early the next day, the coyote told us that the Border Patrol agents changed shifts at around seven o'clock and that they don't even pay attention to who goes across. He was right. We crossed without any difficulty. Some people-wait for us at a junkyard auto shop. They put me under the seat, and my sister went as a passenger in the front seat.

That's how we reached a house in San Diego. A gringo

who stepped out of a black car speaking very good Spanish asked, "How many pollos did you bring?"

"Just these two." He handed him the money, and they ordered us to get into the trunk of the black car.

The gringo took us to another house in Santa Ana. Another coyote would be responsible for taking us to look for the Mexican-American who had left us high and dry in Tijuana.

"We're going to sleep in a motel, and we'll go looking for the old man who owes you guys money early tomorrow," he told us.

We arrived at a motel, and they gave us a room with a living room and a bedroom.

"You sleep out here, and your sister and I will sleep in the bedroom," he told me.

He had already started to walk away when I grabbed him by the arm. "What? You think I was born yesterday? Or, do you think that I would actually allow you to have your way with her?"

"Don't get all uppity with me," he warned. "If we don't find that old man, I'm going to send you back to your god-forsaken country."

"Sure you will," I retorted. "You and your pack of coyotes are going to pay for us to go back home," I challenged him. "I don't care if you do send us back, because I'll call the police so you and your gang can go to jail."

We were on the verge of throwing blows when my sister intervened. I sat on the bed. The coyote calmed down, too. I suggested that we go look for the Mexican-American at that very moment.

"Here, I have his address and license plate number."

"Whoa!" said the coyote. "You're not as dumb as I thought."

It was already late at night when we arrived at his place

of residence. A very short, round woman greeted us. She was the manager of the building. She informed us that the man we were looking for had moved, and she didn't know his new address. I had the gut feeling that she did. I walked away from the coyote, and I told her privately, "You know what, ma'am? My story is too long to tell you, but our lives are in danger. We have no time to lose. This man is a coyote. He wants to rape my sister and he has threatened to send us back if we can't find the man who left us stranded in Tijuana. He has to give this coyote the money he stole from me."

She wrote down the address on a piece of paper. "Good luck," she said as she handed it over to me.

We decided to look for the Mexican-American on the following day. We were too tired, and we hadn't eaten anything all day.

The next day, we waited for him until he left his apartment. We stopped him before he got in his car. He was surprised to see us. Without giving him time to react, I jumped on top of him. "You crook! You son of a bitch! Give us our money back!"

The coyote also intervened, "Come on, you son of a bitch, give him his money back!"

We both beat him up. The Mexican-American took out the money in a hurry. The coyote snatched it away from him, and I continued to hit him. The coyote grabbed me so that I would let him go. I continued to insult him. We went back for my sister, and the coyote dropped us off on a street in downtown Los Angeles, where we took a bus to Hollywood.

By the next day, I was working at my old job again. After a few days, my sister found work in a house where she was able to live. It took us a year to pay off the debt that we took on in order to come.

Months went by, and I began to write my girlfriend regularly. One morning I decided that I should go back for my girlfriend. News of the war arrived sporadically. Whenever some foreigner died, the news was filled with details on the front page of the newspapers. El Salvador also started to make the news on television. The world had its sights set on my little country, my tiny country. Civilian casualties were increasing. Ronald Reagan announced more military aid to El Salvador.

I got married in the middle of the noise from the bombardments. There was no music, only good wishes. The streets were in ruins. Families torn apart. Many of my friends were dead. They had admitted my sister at a hospital in Los Angeles: so many emotions all at once had put a strain on her heart. She needed an operation immediately. I felt guilty for having left her alone, but my girlfriend's life was at stake.

We were wed on November 9, 1985. We went to the embassy to try to acquire a visa. They refused to give us one. I told the official, "You know what? We're gonna go there, anyway. So, see-ya!"

We located an agency that guaranteed us trips to the United States twenty-four hours a day. They gave us a date of departure, and they got us passports with visas to Mexico. The national holiday in El Salvador was drawing near. In spite of the danger, people were preparing to observe it with a mass demonstration. That day, the bombardments intensified. The government could count on help from the United States. There were aerial attacks with sophisticated fighter planes that were hard to distinguish. The noise was deafening. The fear of dying. All of us lying down on the ground. The bombs falling closer and closer: boom, boom, boom. Three, four, five, we counted up to fifteen. We spent the whole night like that. Fully dressed, lying on the floor. In the morning, everyone went out into the streets. Few neighbors remained. We all looked scared. We couldn't believe so much destruction. The place where the day before there had been houses, schools, store, a bank. Everything had disappeared. All that was in front of us were ruins. Many people were killed and many more injured. Death and chaos had seized control of all of the towns, all of the cities. We left that same day. My father-in-law encouraged us: "You're young, just like my daughter. You're in danger. Get out as soon as you can."

We went to Mexico City by plane, then took another one to Tijuana. They came by for us in a van that same evening. They dropped us off in a virtual wasteland. Without thinking about it, we crossed the border by lifting the metallic fence on the dividing line. We ran with the coyote in the lead. My wife didn't recognize the danger; to the contrary, I saw her running happily. For her it was an escape from the tension and the danger of dying each day. We continued to run until the coyote screamed, "Get down!" We obeyed.

Not a sound could be heard. Suddenly, a scream startled us. "I saw you already. I'm going to call the Border Patrol, you wetbacks!" a gringa woman shouted hysterically.

Nobody moved. A short time went by. We still didn't move. In complete silence, we waited for a sign from the coyote. Two officers came by. The horses' gallops could be heard nearby. "Nobody move. And don't say a word," the coyote warned us.

The uniformed officers passed by. A second race. Some gang members were waiting for us to come down the hill. They put us in their car. Hidden, they took us to an Anglo man's house. There, we joined up with other undocumented people. I counted more than fifty. They had spent over two days in that house; they were waiting for a diesel truck to arrive.

Three young ladies told us how the coyotes had raped them. They confessed to us that later they had been forced to submit themselves to the coyotes voluntarily, because they needed the money. The following day, an enormous semi arrived full of boxes of tomatoes. One of the coyotes moved the boxes over to one side and showed us the hole. There were about eighty of us. We all fit. A lady who was wearing like ten changes of clothes kept taking them off one by one over the course of the trip. The heat was suffocating. The truck driver stopped at the inspection depot. We heard noises. They opened the back door. At that moment, we all stopped breathing. We heard laughter and a lot of chitchat. It gave me the impression that everything had been arranged. The driver continued on to Los Angeles. Once there, he parked in front of a house and ordered us to get out and go into the house. My wife put her hands on her head. "Oh! It hurts! It hurts!"

"What's wrong?" I asked her.

"Get me a doctor! A doctor!" she screamed.

"Get a doctor!" I started to shout.

"What's wrong with her?" asked the coyote anxiously.

"I get these attacks."

"Attacks?"

"Yes," she said burying her head in her arms.

"We have to get her to a hospital!" I insisted.

"No," replied the coyote. "Take these two first. I don't want any problems."

We were the first ones to go. The same gang members that picked us up at the bottom of the hill took us to my sister's house. On the way, I realized that the attack that had come over my wife had been feigned.

"Hey, has your pain gone?"

"Yes," she replied.

I held her tightly. A new life awaited us in the United States.

Manuel
Santa Fe Springs, California

All I Thought about Was Disneyland

It's a small world after all
It's a small world after all
It's a small world after all
It's a smaaall, smaaall wooorld!

They dragged him from his house. The boy cried. His bare feet made S's on the ground. His mother called out for help but no one came to her aid. "*Ay*! *Ay*! They're taking my son! They're going to kill him! For the love of God, just let him go!"

Without letting go of the young boy, one of the two officials responded to her with indifference, "It's the law. He must present himself for military service."

"But, sir, he's only twelve years old! He's still a boy!"

"He'll be a man soon enough, ma'am," replied one of the officials. They stopped in front of an armored truck. One of them opened the backdoor, and like a sack of potatoes, they threw the young man inside.

"Murderers! Swine! They're taking my son off to his death!" Like a banshee, Doña Regina, my neighbor from across the street, ran after the truck as it turned the corner.

That was the day my mother made the decision to leave El Salvador along with my seventeen-year-old brother. Two months had gone by since then. The situation grew worse.

The clashes between the army and the guerilla soldiers had become more frequent.

I was one year away from finishing high school. One day I was a student, and the next, in my mother's absence, I had become the woman of the house, at eighteen years of age. I had to cook, clean, iron, and tend to my dad and my five-year-old sister.

When my father shared the news with my little sister, her eyes opened wide. Her cheeks blushed red, and she began to jump for joy. Her dream was coming true. "You and your sister are going to Disneyland." My father's eyes sparkled, and he smiled as if convinced that we were going to meet Pluto and Mickey Mouse.

My little sister couldn't stop laughing. I imagined her in Disneyland, scanning her eyes over the figures of Snow White and the Seven Dwarves. Trembling with excitement at the thought of meeting Mimi and Pocahontas. Television had succeeded in convincing us that Disneyland was a magical paradise.

My father tried to convince me that I needed to leave El Salvador. "Look," he told me. "Remember how they dragged away Doña Regina's son? You know that they would have come for your brother, too. Go, and take your little sister with you. It's too dangerous for you two here," he said with urgency.

I couldn't sleep that night. I went out onto the patio of the house with only my nightshirt on. The moon illuminated the passageway and the ferns than hung from the walls. I breathed in the fragrance of the geraniums, roses, and spikenards. At the end of the patio, there were two *izotes*, whose white flowers scrambled with eggs gave us something to eat in August. It was my mom's favorite little plant. Would there be any *izotes* in the Unites States?

I was a year away from graduating from high school and starting at the university. The violence in El Salvador couldn't go on forever. The end must be near. It was a nation that had been bombarded, broken-down, divided, trod upon, but populated by people who tried to keep happy in the middle of so much suffering. Who would care for the geraniums?

My father was a merchant, and during the week, he traveled to neighboring towns to purchase toys and clothes. On one of those business trips, he disappeared for a number of days. When he returned, he wasn't the same. At night, he was tormented by nightmares. He showed up barefoot and without a shirt on. He had dried, coagulated blood clots stuck to his temples. He had lost many of his teeth in one week. His arms and legs were purple, as if someone had beaten him mercilessly. His body was full of bruises, and it looked like two bracelets had been branded onto his wrists with a hot iron. He spent days in silence, but at night, bits and pieces of what had happened to him escaped from his damaged throat.

"Talk, you son of a bitch! When did you get in from Cuba?"

I would place coldwater compresses on him during his bouts with delirium. I imagined the sinister torturer who interrogated him. "How many of them are there? What's their address?" I thought about his brutal beating. His body hanging from the ceiling, his wrists bound in handcuffs. "Talk, you son of a bitch, or you'll die in here. Where do they keep their weapons?"

My father had been very close to being one of the thousands of missing persons. Only once did he explain how he escaped.

"They threw me out, thinking that I was dead. They stole all of my merchandise." That was the reason why he had decided to send us to the United States.

"We're going to Disneyland! Yippeee!" The memory of my little sister's cries of joy stirred me from my thoughts.

It isn't easy to say good-bye to your country, much less to leave a father who had aged ten years in a week. I was encouraged by the promise that we would all soon be reunited. The farewell was brief. My little sister, excited to see Disneyland, quickly said good-bye. My father took us to the house of the man with whom we would travel. He was a short, thin, dark-skinned man with his head mostly shaved. There were many other people there. He gave us instructions about what we should say in case they stopped us along the way. "Tell them that you came on your own. And when you get off the plane, don't say anything to anyone. Is that clear?" he directed his words to me.

"Yes, sir," I replied.

The airport in Tijuana seemed very small to me. For being such a famous city, everything looked so crowded. The short, dark-skinned man took all of us to a room in a nearby hotel. There, we suffered our first deception. The man opened the door, and the smell of poop and urine almost made me want to throw up. The worst of all was that they had charged us extra money for the quality of the room. He left us all there, locked up, crowded, practically sticking to each other. I smiled at my little sister who looked at me with her very big, very frightened eyes. "From here, they're going to come and take us to Disneyland," I whispered.

Hours went by, long hours full of anguish and anxiety. I peeked out the window. I could make out the hotel marquee: Hotel Catalina. It was beginning to get dark when another man, who was younger than the first but had some gray hair around his temples and his hair almost down to his shoulders, appeared. His gaze left me petrified. He had the look of a lecherous animal. He took us to a house. It smelled just as bad as, or maybe even worse than the hotel room. It was an ugly, abandoned house very close to the fence separating Mexico from the United States. We stayed there for the rest of the night. The man with gray hair left and then came back with sandwiches that had more chile on them than anything else. My little sister ate hers without complaining. All that we had in our stomachs were the candy and nuts that they had given us on the plane.

The noises from the street passed through the cracks in that really ugly house. Howling dogs and wailing police sirens sounded like they were very close. My blood began to race through my veins. I propped myself up against the wall and sat my little sister on my lap. I dozed all night long. I saw myself among the geraniums and the spikenards in my house in El Salvador, the ring of ferns covering my shoulders, my battered father treating his injuries, illuminated by the round, milky moon. I hadn't left El Salvador. I was in my bed; I was getting ready to start at the university. This wasn't happening.

I opened my eyes. My little sister was asleep. My legs had gone numb. I looked at her. Her curls fell onto her forehead. The red ribbon that held her hair in place this morning had now fallen onto her shoulders. A shout startled her. Two figures in the doorway. One of them was coming in our direction. "C'mon, you bunch of lazy bums, wake up," he said with indifference. There was no emotion in his voice. I could make him out better. Where there wasn't gray, his hair was dark brown, his eyes very black with very long eyelashes. Thin lips, he wouldn't stop staring at me.

The man who had been with us since El Salvador was also looking at me. As I woke my little sister up, he approached me. He sat on an imaginary bench with his elbows on top of his knees. "Stay by my side at all times." He spoke in a gentle, paternal tone.

It was starting to get dark when we left the house. They took us to a far-off place. It was like an open field, but there weren't any trees. They made us walk toward the mountains. I had never walked so much in my life. I worked hard to keep myself close to the man who had spoken to us with such a fatherly voice. We must have walked for a number of hours. The swelling on my feet showed it.

Out of the shadows, a group of motorcyclists jumped out and surrounded us. It was a large circle. The lights from the motorcycle riders blinded us momentarily: zzzoooommmm, zzzzooooommmmm. The circle closed around us. They looked like rabid dogs circling their prey. They drove their motorcycles with dexterity. They dodged the shrubs with precision. My little sister clung onto my legs. Who were those men with hate in their eyes? Their clothing was just like in the movies. Black jackets, black gloves that showed their naked fingers. I looked all around. It was as if we had climbed to the top of a hill. The tension was growing. Then one said something to our guides. Without delay, the younger one handed him a paper bag. Without turning off his motorcycle, he made a sign, and they all returned to the shadows from whence they came. Everything happened so fast that I still wonder if it all wasn't just a dream.

We crossed a ravine when I felt the hand of the man with graying hair on my little sister's shoulder. I looked at him surprised. He apologized, saying that he just wanted to help me with her. I hesitated before letting her go. It was his first friendly gesture toward me. He hugged my little sister. I walked along next to her, holding her hand. The man panted from the effort and stared at me in a strange manner. A cold sweat began to run down my spine. The hike became harder and longer. I asked him to give her back to me. I was going to take her by the hand. I had her next to me when somebody yelled, "The Border Patrol!"

I felt my blood race through my veins. Everyone took off running. Without letting go of my little sister's hand, I hid behind some shrubs. The rest did the same. I could hear helicopters above, and a blinding light came from the sky. We stayed hidden in the shrubs. A shadow approached and reached for my little sister. I thought I was going to go crazy. When I came out, I couldn't see her anywhere. Twenty minutes went by. They were the longest twenty minutes of my life. The immigration officers hadn't seen us. All were coming out from their hiding places except for the man who had helped me with my little sister. I was about to scream when he came out from some shrubs with her. I embraced her, and we both started to cry. At that moment, the coyote with black eyes and graying hair told the man who had taken us out of El Salvador, "The young lady and the little girl are coming with me."

I peed on myself, I was so scared. There were thirty of us in the group.

"They're coming with me, right?"

I went silent.

"The only person who's going to go with you is your fucking mother," the other one replied.

Upon hearing this, the Mexican coyote let loose on the Salvadoran and whacked him with a punch. He fell on his back. I felt a pit in my stomach. The Salvadoran coyote got back to his feet and went after him with such rage that the Mexican coyote screamed, "Chill out, dumbass, because if you don't, you can go to hell!"

"Calm down, man, if you know what's good for you."

"I know what's good for *you*."

"I guess we can go together," replied the Salvadoran.

The two looked at each other like rabid dogs. They exchanged blows. Finally, the Mexican coyote said, "You can just die here, for all I care. But I'm warning you, I'm not going to help them. You have five minutes to make it across that open space and reach the other side of the highway." His black eyes had swollen up from the beating.

We waited for the sign for all of us to start running. When the man who had defended us wasn't looking, the Mexican coyote drew his rough face up to mine. "You and your little sister aren't going to make it." My pulse accelerated. A moment later he yelled, "Now run!"

We all started to run. I wouldn't let go of my little sister's hand. The run turned into a race full of obstacles, declines, narrow passageways, until we came to an esplanade with few trees. My God! It was awful! There, they ordered us to lie down on the ground. My little sister and I shook from head to toe. After quite a while, the sound of a car could be heard. It was a van. They shoved us inside in such a hurry that they threw my little sister inside as if she was some kind of inanimate object. We were all sitting on top of each other. They took us to a house in San Diego. I realized that all of the houses that the coyotes used had the same smell: urine, excrement, and vomit. They told us to sleep on the floor. The Mexican coyote stared at me and licked his lips with a mocking smile. There were already two other women waiting in that house. Now there were more than thirty of us.

Sitting down, with my back straight, sore, up against the wall, with my little sister sleeping on top of my legs, I closed my eyes. I saw the volcanoes, the passageway full of ferns, and I breathed in the fragrance of the spikenards. The man who had taken care of us noticed that I was awake. He sat down beside me. He spoke to me quietly, "Remember, your father sent you here so that you could have a better life. And your little sister, too. Very early tomorrow morning we leave for Los Angeles. The hard part is all over." I thanked him for having looked after us. He told me about all of the nice things in the United States. "People obey the law here, my dear. For running a stop sign, they fine you about the equivalent of 500 colones."

We were greeted by cloudy skies in Los Angeles. My little sister, disconcerted, asked, "Are we in Disneyland yet?"

Angélica
Los Angeles, California

We Arrived at the Town of "Thank God"

I was born in Peru, where I graduated with a degree in education, but worked as a cab driver. I was working twelve hours a day. I had saved $1,800 to buy myself a car. I only needed another $500 for the down payment when I received the call that would change my life forever. It was my cousin Paul. It had been ten years since he had left Peru to go to the United States. He encouraged me to join him. Though I told him no at first, I later changed my mind.

When I told my wife about the trip, she began to cry like a little girl. I had known her since she was very young. I was able to convince her to allow me to make the trip. When I talked to my parents, they didn't like the idea either, especially my mother. But, just like my wife, I was able to convince her, too. The hardest part came later: I had to say good-bye to my young son. I think I could sense something, that perhaps it would be a long time before I saw them again.

I left on July 4, the United States's Independence Day. What a day to go! We arrived at the airport two hours before the plane's scheduled departure for Panama. I embraced my mother and my wife. I looked at my son. I took him to the bathroom, and I spoke to him as if he were a man, even though he was only six years old. I told him that, in my absence, he would be the man of the house; I was going to go far away, and he needed to take good care of his mother. The time of departure drew near. My mother began to cry. I felt a strange sensation pass through my heart that I couldn't explain. My wife held me, but I didn't see her cry. I whispered in her ear that she needed to be strong in front of my mother. My son looked at me, and I hugged him. I turned around toward the security gate. They still had to inspect my luggage. I turned around again, and I realized that I had walked down a long corridor; my family was long gone. I continued to walk and didn't see them again.

I told myself over and over again that this was the right decision. I was leaving in order to make a better life for my family. It was for the good of everyone: for my son, for my wife, and for my entire family. I arrived in Panama at eleven o'clock in the morning on July 4. I stayed in Panama for two days. I was issued a visa to cross into Costa Rica. It was good for thirty days. I remained in Costa Rica for twenty days, because they didn't want to grant me a visa to enter Nicaragua. A Peruvian coyote took me all the way to Guatemala. We crossed the border by walking through some mountains; after three hours, we reached a place called Rivas; we took the bus to Managua from there. In Managua, I ditched the Peruvian coyote because we weren't making any progress. He had promised me that it would take us three days to reach Managua, but it had taken two weeks. A coyote from Honduras took me to the Honduran border around five o'clock in the afternoon without any delay.

On the following day, we left at about four in the morning on our way to Tegucigalpa, and from there, to the Salvadoran border. In El Salvador, we ate some tacos and rested for a few hours. We crossed the river joining El Salvador with Guatemala at one in the morning. After fording the river, we hiked for about three hours then took a bus to

Guatemala City. We reached the Guatemalan capital at around three o'clock in the afternoon. We ate lunch in the town. I took advantage of the opportunity to call my cousin Paul's in-laws. He was married to a woman from Guatemala, and his in-laws were living there.

I stayed in Guatemala for two months. I worked as a painter and a door-to-door salesman, because I had run out of money. At the time, it cost $2,500 to get from Guatemala to the United States. My cousin Paul sent me money to complete the journey. There were Central Americans, Ecuadorians, and Hindus on that trip. I was the only Peruvian. We arrived at the Tecuman border. There, we were packed into a giant sewage pipe; there were approximately sixty of us: children, adults, and old people.

The federal police discovered us in Oaxaca, Mexico, and they sent us back. We tried to cross once again through a Mexican town by the name of "Gracias a Dios" (Thank God) which was located in the state of Chiapas. We were there for almost two weeks, eating only one meal a day. After that, we were loaded into a large tractor-truck trailer. There were around 120 people. The only food that we had for the whole trip was a can of Jumex fruit juice, some cookies, and an apple. We felt like animals, like sheep on their way to slaughter. Before closing the door, they gave us two plastic buckets for our necessities. I was the first to use one of them. I didn't know if I was doing it because I wanted to serve as an example or because I was afraid that I wouldn't be able to use them later.

When we left Chiapas, they gave us a few tortillas along with the meat of an animal that I couldn't identify with any certainty. And, even though I was very hungry, the meal didn't sit well with me.

We arrived in Mexico City at around two o'clock in the morning. The trip had taken more than a day to complete.

Mexico City was the only place where they treated us like human beings. A man and his wife, whom they called "The Güera," attended to us for two days in their very own home. We parted in groups of eighteen. And as luck would have it, I was in the first group to go. We traveled by bus to Tamaulipas, and from there, we took a train to Agua Prieta, Sonora. Along the way, the federal police boarded the bus, but we weren't worried. They had already explained to us that all we needed to do was give them two hundred pesos and say, "We're with The Güera."

The Güera traveled with us. And each time they took our two hundred pesos, she came around and provided us with another two hundred pesos to continue on our way. During one of these inspections, in a place called Torreón, Coahuila, two Dominican women were taken off the bus and weren't allowed to get back on board. We never learned what happened to them. Two days of traveling and handing two hundred pesos to every group of federal police that stopped our bus to pass inspection had gone by. It took almost three days to reach the city of Agua Prieta, where they took us to a house where more than two hundred people were staying. We spent three days there and then moved to a town that was across the border from Phoenix, Arizona.

I clearly recall that it was October 31, at noon, when we left inside a garbage truck. There were approximately forty people. They dropped us off in a deserted area with three guides: one in front, another in the middle of the group, and the third one near the rear. We walked most of the way, but we were forced to run whenever they instructed us to do so. There were women who couldn't run because they were carrying babies in their arms.

An Ecuadorian man and I took responsibility for carrying a small boy. We each held one arm each. When I looked at the young boy, he reminded me of my own son. They were about the same age. One of the guides told me to leave him with his mother. He informed me that if the Border Patrol were to catch me with a child, they could charge me with the smuggling of a minor. I got scared and returned him to his mother.

At around five o'clock in the afternoon, after we had walked for so many hours, one of the guides told us that we were now in the United States. We had to wait for the night to fall. It was terribly cold, but that didn't matter because a few trucks suddenly arrived. We left in groups of twelve. I was in the second group. The drive took about three hours. The cold grew more intense. We reached Phoenix at close to three in the morning. The coyote who welcomed us was Peruvian. He permitted me to speak with my cousin. Paul came for me on the following day and paid the coyote what he had owed him. I felt very lucky. In the Peruvian's house, I had met people who had been there for more than a month because their families still couldn't collect the money that they needed to take them home.

Freddy
Los Angeles, California

A Honeymoon on the Road

Your way of loving me
is to let me love you.
The "yes" you use to win me over
goes unspoken. Your kiss
is to offer me your lips
so that I can kiss them myself.
—Pedro Salinas

Living in the United States was never in my plans, much less marrying someone who lived to the north of Mexico. I learned from my aunts' experiences, plump women, always waiting for a love letter, lonely eyes peering through windows, nights of insomnia filled with longing. I refused to be like them: trapped, unable to have any male friends for fear of being accused of infidelity and of their husbands being called cuckolds. My aunts were pretty, and they had been married in white wedding dresses.

I wasn't going to be like them, a wife subjected to a lifetime of waiting. *I don't know what's on your lips, I don't know what's in your eyes, that takes control of my whimsy and makes my heart go crazy.* Devoted to the memory of the man she loves but having no one by her side. *At night, when I awaken, I ask the heavens to forget you, but by morning, when I wake, I live only to adore you.*

I told him "no" three times before agreeing to dance with him for one song. *Your lips are so powerful that when they kiss me I tremble . . .* His strong hands holding my waist. The music smooth, caressing, *and they make me feel like both slave and master of the universe.* I hadn't noticed when the band stopped playing the song that my aunts used to sing. We stayed out on the dance floor, holding hands. The next song was fast, but we danced close. *When I was just a lad, my mama told me to look for love, nothing but love.*

I had refused to dance with him because of his newcomer-from-the-north appearance: the cowboy hat, the boots that looked like they were too heavy to walk in. But, on the dance floor, he was light on his feet. He told me about his life alone in Los Angeles. *Don't look for a pretty love, said she, because as time passes her beauty will no longer be.* It had been ten years since he had moved from León, Guanajuato. He was ready to start a family. *Look for love, nothing but love.* His heart was telling him that the mother of his children was standing right in front of him, he told me. I laughed nervously. This stranger seemed to be a little too forward. A mixture of curiosity and vanity kept me listening to him. He had an average-looking face; his laugh was quick, noisy like a child's. We agreed to see each other on the following day; and two weeks later, we were engaged to be married. I refused to follow my aunts' examples. I would have a warm body in my bed every night. A body that I could press up to mine. I refused to live on nostalgia, nor would I be left back at home.

We were married one fine day in May, and still dizzy from the wedding, we departed for Tijuana. The entire family came out to bid us farewell, including my aunts, who never stopped crying about my departure. I was very excited to see Tijuana. Everyone in Guanajuato talked about the city. I imagined it to be a metropolis full of glass skyscrapers, its streets clean and orderly. This is the way it must look because of its proximity to the United States. Traveling by airplane was a pleasant experience. From up high, a row of cardboard houses could be seen. That could not be Tijuana.

The reality of the city hit me with the same intensity as colic in wintertime. We drove through the civic center in a taxi that we took from the airport. The strength of my husband's arms rested on my shoulders. The city was sordid. The houses were ugly. There were child panhandlers begging for money on the street corners. Dogs sniffed around the trashcans. It was the same grief and despair that I had seen in Mexico City. A little girl strummed a guitar with only three strings. Another girl, who could have been no more than five years old, shook a pair of discolored maracas and sang . . . *And since I didn't speak any English, they shipped us out to Juárez . . . The Border Patrol got me again . . .*

"C'mon, lady, give me enough to get a taco. My little sister and I haven't eaten. *Two hundred times a wetback*," she told me between the verses of her song.

The taxi driver looked at them with indifference. My husband took out a coin and placed it in her hand. The stoplight changed, and off we went.

The taxi driver dropped us off at the coyote's house, where we received our first bad news. He had gone on vacation, and they didn't know when he was going to be back. That was the first day of our honeymoon. We dined on canned food and fresh vegetables that we bought at a store.

Tijuana didn't turn out to be like I had imagined it, but I knew that the United States would be just as I had seen it on television. Pictures don't lie. It's a country full of beautiful, well-dressed people, a life full of comfort and convenience. People must live very well there because entire towns have emigrated there. I pictured Hollywood: a city full of lights, stars dressed in furs that cost too much. An assiduous reader of *Selecciones Reader's Digest*, I had fallen in love with the United States' fine customs. I knew about their orderly lifestyle and their thoughtfulness for others. I recalled a particular article about how people greeted each other in the streets with a simple "hi." "Hospitality and consideration are characteristic of American society," the article read.

I was excited about the idea of being able to go see a Bee Gees concert. I had a complete collection of their songs. I had watched the movie *Saturday Night Fever* five times just for the music. I was one of the first ones to buy their records when they arrived at Discoteca Silvia in Guanajuato. They had all of their songs: "More than a woman," "How deep is your love." "If I can't have you" was my favorite. But, even though I was crazy for the Bee Gees' music, the person who I really wanted to see in concert was Santana. I knew the lyrics to his songs by heart: *Oye cómo va, mi ritmo vamos a gozar, ta, ta, ta.* When I talked about my musical tastes with my husband on the airplane, I realized that we were very different. He preferred the music of bands like Los Buquis and Los Tigres del Norte.

His cousin Juan arrived at the room where we were staying. My husband had informed him about our wedding and our desire to move to the United States. His cousin Juan decided to come along and help. He took us to the place where we could go across without being spotted by the Border Patrol. There was an enormous wall in front of us. I didn't know how we were ever going to get across. Standing in front of that wall, it seemed strange to me that the very same land could be divided with such suspicion.

Juan said that we should cross through Tecate, so we headed off in that direction. We found ourselves in front of an enormous barbed-wire fence. Juan suggested that we continue to walk along the side of the fence. As we moved forward, we noticed huge holes dug under the fence. As we walked by, we discovered precarious dwellings each made out of four sticks and a piece of cardboard for a roof. Whole families stared at us with hungry eyes.

After a number of hours, my husband noticed a huge hole on one side of the fence; it was like a deep crevice. We peeked in. There were about thirty people inside. Their hair and checks were covered with dirt. The coyote identified himself to us. The men came to an agreement: he would take us across as well.

We made ourselves comfortable in the crevice, which seemed to be much narrower to me once inside. In only a few minutes, our hair and cheeks were covered with dirt, too. I snuggled up to my husband. I cuddled up in his arms. He rested his chin on my head. There wasn't a lot of room for moving around. A few minutes went by. Inside, there were two women with children in their arms. One of the babies started to cry. The child's wailing was heartbreaking. It was crying from hunger. The emaciated woman, almost corpselike, lifted her sweater. Two limp breasts dropped out; then she began to breastfeed her child, who desperately started to suck on her nipple. The silence was absolute. The other woman looked at her nervously. The men looked away. The baby's screaming broke the silence. The child became restless. The other woman intervened: "Give him here. I'll fill him up for you." The emaciated woman held out the baby in her arms. She lowered her head to hide the tears that came rolling down her cheeks.

Neither one of the women wore a brassiere. The scene played itself over again. The emaciated woman showed her limp breasts, and the one who sat next to her, a woman who was not so thin, with short hair, a cleft chin, and a distinguished beauty, wound up taking the baby away from her in order to nurse him herself. Unlike the emaciated woman, she had round, refulgent, inviting breasts.

The sun had gone gray when the coyote told us to come out: a few at first, then all the others. He gave us instructions about how we should run across. We would crawl across a green pasture and not stop until he gave us the signal.

If I can't have you, I don't want nobody, baby, if I can't have you, oh, oh, oh, the song went with me the whole time that I was running and followed me while we crawled on our bellies like snakes on an open plain. The coyote whispered, "We'll have to slip by the Border Patrol that keeps watch from up on the hill."

My husband looked at me with concern. I continued to crawl. The women moved forward, kneeling down and with babies in their arms. My eyes burned. We continued to advance until an authoritative voice was heard: "Everyone stop. *No mover nadie*."

The order had come from a patrol vehicle that had come out from the shadows and moved towards us. We threw ourselves on the ground and onto a puddle of mud. I covered my head with my hands. The sound from the vehicle could be heard. It got closer and closer, as if they were going to run over me. I closed my eyes. The noise from the engine caused me to recoil. The tire was a foot and a half from my head. My husband ran to lift me to my feet. I felt as though he had lifted the entire weight of my body completely off the ground.

We were the only ones arrested. All of the others were able to escape. The officer called for backup, and another patrol vehicle quickly arrived. During the drive, I thought about my aunts, sitting in their rocking chairs, staring out of their windows at those who pass by. I wanted to be where they were. The patrol vehicle drove a long way, then parked in front of a building.

They separated us when we got out of the car. My husband stretched out his hand to me. He told me not to be afraid.

"*Tú*, follow me." The officer walked quickly, without looking back.

I followed him to the office. It was full of men. The officer walked to the center of the room. I followed him. With his hands on his hips, he turned around in my direction. And, so that everyone could hear, he said out loud, "*Tú*, what're you doing *aquí?* Go on! Get out of here! *Largarte de aquí!*"

I felt my legs tremble. That tall man with flaming red hair was making fun of me. His companions did the same: they laughed, and there I was, wearing wet clothes, with my hands and elbows covered in mud. It was only three days before that I had been admired in my white wedding dress, my bridesmaids and my groomsmen dressed in satin and velvet. I wanted to spit in his freckled face. I turned around and stormed out, indignant.

They deported me and my husband to Tijuana. It surprised me to see how natural it was for the people who saw us in the street. It was as if our appearance was something common in that city. Two days went by, and we found another coyote; this one was much younger than the one before. We would pass through Tecate. When reaching the metallic fence, a young man of about fourteen or fifteen years of age approached us. Another guy who was a little older than he was accompanied him. The teen stepped forward to the hole where we had been just a couple of days earlier. He slipped through with great ease. From there, he yelled back to the coyote, "*¡El mosco!*"

"Everybody down!" shouted the coyote.

We took a big leap into a rich pasture. I was surprised that we weren't hurt from the impact. It was ten o'clock at night. It started to rain. Once again, we started to run and crawl on our bellies like soldiers. It was a long way. We crossed a bridge that turned out to be a drainage line under the highway. The coyote and the teen went up a hill. My husband took advantage of the moment to tell Juan, who had caught up to us, "If they try anything on us, you take the little guy and I'll get the other one."

The coyote called us over. We went up the hill. He pointed out a patrol vehicle that seemed to have spotted us and was coming our way. The coyote showed us a road; we followed it. We jumped a fence. We trespassed on private property. Fortunately, the patrol vehicle drove away. We walked for three hours. We experienced a very difficult moment when we crossed some cliffs and rocky mountains. When we climbed down from one of them, we found ourselves surrounded by bulls and cows. There were about a thousand head of cattle. I was paralyzed with fear. The coyote told us to keep walking, and show no signs of fear. We were able to reach the back end of the fence. We hopped over it without frightening the cattle. My feet felt swollen and numb. The young kid tried to encourage me. I supported myself on him. My husband appeared to be jealous: "I never told you that it was going to be easy. You should have done more exercise."

I didn't say anything. I just tried to go on without the young man's assistance. Juan offered to help me.

"Why doesn't any of this happen on television?" I wondered. No one ever talks about it, either. All we know is that the United States is very beautiful and that people make a lot of money there. At least that's what the people who come from up north say. I began to suspect that the television had lied to me, too.

The coyotes nimbly crossed the mountains. I made an effort not to faint due to exhaustion. Out of the corner of my eye, I observed how my husband was following me at a short distance. He had aged overnight. His eyes were sunken. We had not eaten anything all day.

A light rain began to make things even more difficult for us on our walk. As we advanced, the rain became more intense. The heavy drops fell like rocks upon our backs. I took off my shoes. My knees were shaking, and it felt as though my feet were stepping on tacks.

The coyote pointed out a few factories that could be made out further ahead. To get there, we had to cross a few drainage ditches. I fought back the nausea because the coyote called for complete silence. I felt my blood throbbing in my temples. I felt like throwing up. Was this my honeymoon? My husband appeared very distant. The fatigue had gotten to him as well.

We came out to one side of the factory. The barking of dogs could be heard. It was two o'clock in the morning, maybe three. We kept going until we reached a warehouse. We hid under some stairs; we stayed there until the morning. I fell asleep. Various male voices woke me up. The young man told me that we were in Chula Vista, and that the employees were beginning to arrive. That city must have been very far from Tijuana because we had walked a long way.

Very mysteriously, the coyote called us over, separate from the others. He instructed us to walk over to a nearby grove. We did as he said. A man in a red car was waiting for us there. We waited for a few minutes. The coyote, Juan, and the young man joined us. The man turned the keys and quickly drove off. They put my husband and his cousin in the trunk. They hid me under the backseat. The coyote drove, and the young man sat next to him. After driving for a little while, I heard the car come to a stop. A man gave some clothing to the coyote and took the young man with him. He started the car again. We made a second stop, where he made me sit up front. We made it through the inspection without any problem. "We slipped by them! We're safe now!" I thought to myself.

I could see everything from the front seat. The houses all looked the same. The new cars. The street signs. Bob Hope

Dr., I read. I never knew Bob Hope was a doctor, too. Other artists also had "Dr." at the end of their names. I later learned that "Dr." stood for "Drive." At that moment, I thought about Hollywood. Behind me was the ugly, the grotesque, and the malodorous. I looked forward to finishing my interrupted honeymoon with my husband who was riding in the trunk. A Santana concert, and why not? one by the Bee Gees and a visit to Hollywood.

If I can't have you, I don't want nobody baby, if I can't have you, oh, oh, oh. The coyote looked at me like I was crazy. I didn't care. I kept on singing. I was happy.

Fabiola
Los Angeles, California

A Discount for Telling the Truth

The news spoke about one hundred thousand refugees who had crossed the border from Guatemala to Mexico. The news also spoke about the incursions met by the army in Chiapas and about the indigenous people who had died. I wasn't planning on staying in Mexico, nor was I going to take my family as refugees. I would go to the United States first, and then I would send for them. Guatemala had become a very difficult place to live. Lashed and beaten by death, we farm workers, rather than tilling the earth for corn spent our time filling it with dead bodies. The struggle for land was becoming fierce. The landowners provoked the farm workers to kill one another. No one knew whether or not his own neighbor would decide to kill him on the following day. The green fields of Guatemala had been converted into cemeteries. Human remains became confused with the bones of the animals. There was no other choice: leave or die.

I'm writing about this because few understand the circumstances under which people lived in Guatemala, mainly during the seventies and eighties. To the world, Guatemala was little more than a poor country, perhaps one of the poorest in the world. They still have that image to this very day.

I made an arrangement with a friend to leave together, along with his two sisters, on December 28. Leaving Guatemala was very sad. His two sisters pressed their faces against the windows. We were leaving a fertile land, rich with resources, but full of inequalities as well. I loved that land of deer, coyotes, gophers, and wild *chompipe* turkeys. But I had to leave it behind in order to be able to live and get ahead with my family.

I made my concerns clear to them along the way. "Hey, where are we going, anyway?"

"To Tijuana. You can hire a coyote there."

"Do you already have one in mind?"

"There'll be plenty. They're everywhere."

"Do you have to pay first?"

"No. You pay once you're on the other side."

"I hope things go well for us."

"Don't worry. We'll get there."

My friends words put me at ease. His sisters were sitting in the seats on the sides. They pointed out trees, plants, and mountains during the whole stretch of the way. At times, they would quietly snicker covering their mouths. It gave me the impression that they were telling each other stories to dispel their fears.

We reached the border with Mexico. We showed them our Guatemalan passports. An immigration officer asked us, one by one, "Where are you going?"

Almost everyone responded: "To Mexico City."

"To Tijuana," I said.

The man threw his arms up to the air and exclaimed: "Wow! Finally, someone who is telling the truth!" Speaking to all of us, he said, "You see? This gentleman is the only one who told the truth. All of you are headed to Tijuana. And if you want me to let you get through, you already know what you have to do."

We all paid. The officer collected our money so naturally. When he came to me, I put out twenty-five dollars for him.

"No, sir. Just give me fifteen."

He gave me a discount for telling the truth. I was free to go. We boarded a bus going to Mexico City. We made ourselves comfortable in our seats. Then we had another setback. Another inspector appeared at the door of the bus. We had just paid one of them. It was the same questions. He started with those who sat in the front seats.

"How much money do you have?"

The quantities varied: 200, 300, 250, 400. He was standing next to where we were seated. My friend asked, "Why do you want to know?"

The question infuriated him. "I am the inspector. You have to answer."

"I'm carrying five hundred dollars in my shoes," my buddy said.

"Let me see it. And if you don't do it immediately, I'll kick you off the bus right here."

My friend was about to take it out when the officer started to yank on his arm. Surprised, he raised his eyes. "Look, I'm going to show you the money."

Without any reply, he pulled him by the arm to drag him off the bus. His two sisters got up from their seats. They ran toward him, crying. "That's our brother! Where are you taking him? Sir, please, if you send us back, they'll kill us! Just let us go!"

The image that I still have of my friend is that of the tremendous hate in his face, motionless before his sisters, who begged the Mexican immigration official to allow them to continue on their way. "If we go back, they'll kill us!" The officer's expression did not change. With a glacial frigidity, he callously ordered for them to be returned to Guatemala. I never heard from them again.

That was my first adverse experience. I knew nothing about Tijuana. The trip lasted a whole night and the entire next day. We came to a very big plaza where there were terminals for various bus companies that traveled to different cities in Mexico. I took a bus on the Tres Estrellas bus line destined for Tijuana. The bus slid softly over the asphalt. There were no clouds in the sky. It was a sunny day. I was able to admire the various landscapes, large stretches of land, lush forests followed by rows of mountain.

The night fell quickly on the road. Conversations became increasingly scarce. Guadalajara was only a short distance away. Guadalajara made such an impression on me, with its churches, its streets, its monuments. How I longed to see it on foot like the tourists that I saw through the window. We passed very close to the cathedral. On one side, I saw tourists riding in horse-drawn carriages. The bus driver parked downtown for a little while. We ate at a small restaurant with a large menu. All of the dishes made my mouth water: beef covered in green chili sauce, beef covered in red chile sauce, chiles in a spicy walnut sauce, breaded chiles, torta sandwiches smothered in chile sauce. I quickly realized that whatever I ordered was going to come with chile. I decided on the smothered torta sandwich. The spicy burning sensation lasted the whole day and part of the next one.

The bus driver accelerated as he hit the highway on the way to Nayarit, our second stop. The bus chewed up the miles at high speeds. During our brief stops, all kinds of vendors would approach the windows. "Ice cream. Ice cream. Get your ice cream. Iiice creeeam." Panhandlers and vagabonds also put out their hands. The beggars's faces showed the same sad expressions as the indigenous people in Guatemala.

A passenger got up to inquire how long it would take to reach Mexicali. It was the first time I had ever heard the name of that city. He returned to his seat and said out loud, "That checkpoint is tough."

My heartbeat quickened. I asked him about it, and he

told me that before going on to Tijuana, we had to pass through Mexicali and that they detained anyone there who wasn't a Mexican citizen. My heart beat even faster. The man explained that the best thing to do was to make an arrangement with the bus driver. I went up to the bus driver: "Is it hard to make it through the checkpoint in Mexicali?"

"Yeah. Are you crossing to the other side?"

"Yeah. But I'm not sure how to go about it."

"Don't worry. I can help."

I returned to my seat. We drove through Nayarit without stopping. Our next stop was in another fishing village whose name I never learned. I was impressed with its mountains, its tranquil seas. It was truly a beautiful place.

I tried to get some sleep. I don't know how many hours went by, when a tug on the arm woke me up.

"We're just about to enter Mexicali," the same man informed me.

It was cold inside but I started to sweat. Then something unexplainable happened. The bus driver pulled off the highway and got onto a dirt road. The moon illuminated the cacti. The bus continued to advance with some difficulty. The bus driver stopped in front of a cement house surrounded by trees. It was dark all around. The bus driver announced: "I'm going to see my family. I'll be back in a little while." He spoke to us as if it was something very normal.

We all remained quiet, except for a voice that came from the back of the bus: "Hey, pal, I need to take a piss."

"Be my guest. Go out there in the grass," the driver told him and then got off the bus and went inside the house.

Two hours went by, and we were already going on a third. I looked at my watch. It was four minutes after midnight on December 31, 1978. I reminisced about those New Year's eves of my childhood. Sitting together with my brothers in front of the kitchen stove. A pot of tamales cooking over hot *tenamaste* stones. Very close to the cornfields, my father cutting off the ears of corn to cook them up in a high tub that he placed in the middle of the patio. That's how my family appeared to me now: like an ear of corn that was being stripped clean until all that's left is the cob. That's how our land had become, like a corncob, barren and empty.

I missed the aroma of my homeland: *chilacayote* pumpkin seeds, *ayote* squash, the fruit of *achiote* trees, wild *chompipe* turkeys. The barrage of recollections left me grief stricken.

It was New Year's. The bus door opened. The driver boarded the bus with a huge grin on his face. Directing his words to me, he said, "Give me $25 and I'll get you to Tijuana." I gave him the money. The bus started to move again. I don't know how many hours I slept, but when I woke up, the bus had already parked. "We're in Tijuana now," the bus driver informed me.

I walked out of the terminal. The sun was radiant. I looked for a hotel in order to take a shower and change my clothes. Five days went by, and I still hadn't found a coyote who would take me to the other side. I conducted my search very carefully because the Mexican authorities were on the lookout for Central Americans.

On the sixth day, I came across a person who could cross me into the United States. The cyclonic chainlink fence was old and falling apart. It was easy for us to lift it. There were a lot of us. The coyote told us to hide in some small bushes. We squatted there, waiting for our second order.

The propellers of a helicopter flew over our heads. A good while went by. The afternoon faded, and night fell. Around midnight, the annoyed coyote said, "We better go back. The helicopter isn't going to let us move ahead."

I objected. "Let's wait a little longer. It might leave."

"I doubt it. Look at the sky. It's clear. The moon is full.

That helicopter isn't going to let us go anywhere," the coyote warned.

Everyone else took my side and waited there with me. I said a little prayer that my mother taught me when I was a child. *Our Lady, Blessed Mother of God, I beseech thee to help us reach our goal. I feel downtrodden, and my money is dwindling with each passing day, but I implore your blessing.* Not half an hour had gone by before the moon had disappeared. It was a miracle. The sky clouded over, and the helicopter went away when it saw the rain that was falling hard.

"Now's the time! Let's go!" On the coyote's word, we started to run down the hillside. We kept on going until we reached a paved road where a covered van was waiting for us. Further ahead, they made us get out and ordered us to run across the freeway. That's what we did. We came to a sloping hillside but kept going until we reached the beach. Just when we thought that we had made it to our final destination, we realized that we still had a long way to go. We came to a thermonuclear facility and climbed up on one of the hillsides until we reached another highway. There, they picked us up in another vehicle. There were no surprises along the way on the freeway. The coyote took us to a house that was close to Los Angeles. The door was opened by a gray-haired woman wearing thick glasses. I paid her the agreed amount, and I walked out into the street without knowing what I was going to do with my life. I felt like a stranger in a strange land.

Julio
Los Angeles, California

The Old Smoocher

I jumped for joy. I had dreamt of this question so many times that when I heard it over the telephone, I was not able to answer. Something was stuck in my throat.

"Do you want to come and live with me?" she asked again.

"Yes, Mom, of course I do!" I replied.

When you're fourteen years old, you really don't understand much about armed conflict; the one thing that was clear to me was that my life was in danger. The army had taken a number of my friends, and I could be next. The most difficult thing to do was to say good-bye to my grandmother. She had taken care of me in my mother's absence. She had instilled in me a love for El Salvador. She had taught me to have faith that things were going to change. "We can't be at war forever," she would tell me.

But the war continued. The bombardments destroyed everything: the schools, the hospitals, the roads. It seemed as though the war would go on forever.

My grandmother was in the kitchen in front of the stove when I told her the news. She turned around and pretended to be happy. "Well then, my boy, you better start packing."

~ ~ ~

I had my luggage ready, and I was wearing my wool

sweater. I had packed my clothes, my books, and a few photographs. I pushed the curtain over to one side, and a lady with very short hair and blue jeans stepped out of a blue van and approached our home quickly. She was surprised to see me at the door with my bags already packed. "What are you, crazy? You think you're going on vacation? Leave all that there and put on another shirt and another pair of pants over the ones you've got on." I did as I was told.

My grandmother came out to say good-bye. I cried as I embraced her. I kissed her calloused and withered hands. She looked at me. She hugged me and began to fuss, whispering, "Come on, now. Stop your crying. The lady's waiting for you."

I kneeled down at her feet, waiting for her blessing: "In the name of the Father, the Son, and the Holy Spirit. May God and the blessed Virgin Mary protect you on your journey, my boy." I held her just like I did when I was a little boy. It was a desperate embrace, filled with trepidation.

She pushed me away gently. "Give this to your mother, okay?" It was a paper bag. With trembling hands, she placed 200 colones in my hand. "Take this to spend along the way."

The van drove off, and my grandmother remained standing in the middle of the patio, like a tree, firm, erect, with its roots planted deeply into the earth. I regretted not having kissed the wrinkles on her cheeks, not telling her one last time that I loved her very much.

On our way, it dawned on me that I might never see her again, and I couldn't stop crying until something came to frighten away my tears. We had reached the border with Guatemala. We had to take another bus to continue on to Mexico. We were met by a number of soldiers. One of them snatched the paper bag that my grandmother had given me out of my hands. He was disappointed when he discovered that all it had inside was a chunk of cheese. He threw it in the trash. Without asking my permission, he began to rummage through my pants pockets, and he took the money that my grandmother had given me. At the time, I didn't really understand what was taking place. I asked myself how someone could be so cruel that they would humiliate other people in this manner. It took me many years to realize that they, like the soldiers I had left behind in my country and those I would come across in Mexico, were just victims of the same system of corruption. Slaves before their masters, the heads of the military, but masters before the common citizens. The soldiers barely scrape by on their meager salaries, and their ability to keep their jobs depends upon their skills at theft. Soldiers are marginalized members of society who live in the shadow of their tyrannical rulers. They are accessories to fraud and murder. They are creatures that have reduced themselves to the blind obedience of orders from their superiors.

On that particular occasion, I damned them because of the outrage they committed, because they spoke of trivial things while they searched me and robbed me of the little bit of money I had. They permitted the lady and me to leave. A bus was waiting for us to cross into Mexico. I boarded the bus and sat next to the window. Across the aisle from me, there was a woman who would not take her eyes off me. I looked at her, and she smiled. Her lips quivered ever so slightly. It sent a chill down my spine.

There were twenty-five people who embarked on the "cruise." I never learned the name of the city from which the boat set sail. All I knew was that, after almost three days at sea, they would take us from there to the port of Mazatlán, Sinaloa; and from there, we would continue on by bus to Tijuana.

The ship was huge. I could walk on the deck. And I spent all of my time gazing into the sea. I wanted to be the first one to catch a glimpse of the city. It was our second day at sea. The sun was radiant. I was thinking about the United States. I was going to be with my mother; but at the same time, I was tormented by the idea of not being able to see my grandmother. A voice, like that of a young girl, stirred me from my musings. "Why do you look at the sea so much?" It was the woman who had smiled at me on the bus. She had red hair and a big mouth. A small, bleached mustache covered her upper lip. She wore pants that were cut off above the knees. Her legs were shapely, bending over the railing. She asked me provocatively, "So tell me. That lady you're with, is she your mother?"

"No. She's just a friend."

"Don't be ridiculous. That old hag isn't anybody's friend."

I felt a dagger in my back. I wanted to run away, but I couldn't move. She came closer. Her pale, white hand brushing over mine. "You're a very attractive young man, did you know that?"

I began to sweat. The lady who had picked me up at my house in El Salvador suddenly appeared. "Leave him alone! Go find someone your own age."

The woman went away angry. "Enjoy this little cruise, because the worst is yet to come," she informed me.

One more day of waiting went by. The night found me staring into the horizon. A pair of vise-like hands appeared out of nowhere and grabbed my waist from behind. It was the woman with the red hair, who kept repeating, "Don't move. I'm not going to hurt you."

My palms began to sweat, and my throat became dry. Her hands moved about, searching for my belt buckle. I tried to free myself from her clutches, but she was stronger than me. A hot flash washed over me. The woman pressed her body to mine. She made horizontal movements, her hands rummaging below my belt buckle.

I made an effort to break free from her embrace and look at her face to face. She closed her eyes and puckered her lips. I looked at her mustache in disgust. I pushed her to the side and went away running.

The lighthouse in Mazatlán was spotted on the horizon early in the morning. I wanted to be among the first to disembark. The lady who had escorted us all the way from El Salvador stopped me: "Put these clothes on before you get off the boat. You need to look like a tourist."

Wearing a Hawaiian print shirt, shorts, and a pair of sandals, I stepped off the gigantic ship. I looked at everyone else and found it difficult to recognize them. The men wore shorts and Hawaiian shirts. A few had forgotten to remove their socks. Others had inoperable cameras hanging from their necks. I couldn't help but laugh at the entire scene. The fatigue from our lengthy expedition was hidden behind the dark sunglasses that they had given to all of us.

We rested that day from our traveling in order to embark on the journey to Tijuana the following morning. The woman with the mustache took advantage of any possible excuse to try to get close to me. I pretended not to understand her insinuations; and on more than one occasion, I noticed her blowing me kisses. I tried to keep my distance.

The drive to Tijuana took four days. They took us to a house where they divested us of everything that they had loaned to us as well as some of our own personal belongings. That was the second round of looting. It was a large, dirty house that seemed to be raised up on a platform. The floors sounded hollow. In one of the rooms, there was a mountain of stolen goods: clothes, suitcases. That was everything that they robbed from people like us, I thought to myself.

They woke us up very early in the morning, and we left the house on foot. We continued walking, and we didn't stop for a day and a half. I realized that the lady who had picked me up in El Salvador was no longer with us. Our guide was a scrawny, little man; he spoke very little. Late that evening, in a precipice that appeared to have once been a lake, he ordered us to rest. It was a moonless night. Trees, like skeletons, were all around us. I was exhausted, and my legs had become stiff. Noises rose from the dead leaves. "Be careful because there are rats and snakes all around here." I was terrified of snakes, and every sound made me jump with fright.

My weariness forced me to lie down. A rustling of the leaves made me sit back up. I felt it like a bear falling upon its prey, ready to devour it whole, to leave nothing behind. I was paralyzed with fear. I didn't know what it was. It took me a few seconds to realize that the woman with the mustache had jumped on top of me. She tried to kiss me. I covered my mouth with my hand, and she fought back, struggling to hold me still.

At that moment, I forgot all about the snakes and the rats. I don't know where I got the strength to push her away from me. I sprang to my feet and started to run, but with such bad luck that I fell into a hole. I thought that I had broken my leg. I struggled to get up without calling for help. I sat down with another group. The march recommenced before the break of dawn.

I was limping. The pain was so great that I thought I would fall faint, but the fear of the woman who followed closely behind kept me moving forward. A stream of warm liquid trickled down my pant leg. I checked it quickly. It was blood. I didn't care. I continued to walk on pace with the guide. Step for step, stride for stride. We came to a bridge where a pickup with a camper was waiting for us. It was small. It fit ten people, one on top of the other. We drove for about two hours. Then the pickup stopped.

"Get out. You're in the United States," they told us.

Another car took us to another house. They left us there for a night. I situated myself on the sofa, I took off my socks and fell asleep.

When I opened my eyes, I saw that my terrified mother was examining my lacerated feet. My knee was swollen, and blood had dried all over my leg. She cried upon seeing me in such a state. I hugged her, full of emotion. I tried to stand up but I couldn't. They took me to the hospital where they stitched my cut and fixed me up.

I never saw the Old Smoocher again. A week went by, then my mother signed me up for school for the very first time. I was thrilled with the experience of going to school. All that I knew about school I had learned from TV. The big, spacious classrooms. The green playgrounds. The orderly hallways. All of the resources necessary for a student to succeed at one's fingertips. I slept well that night, thinking about the life as a student that awaited me on the following day.

Manuel
Los Angeles, California

It Scared the Tapeworms Out of Her

The Border Patrol showed up, and all of the women in the factory scattered in every direction. One of my friends decided to hide on top of the toilet bowl. She was perched like an eagle, hanging on every sound. She was in that position for so long that a tapeworm squeezed out of her body. When they discovered her, she was trembling and needed help to get down because she was so numb. If it were not for the gravity of the situation, we would have been hysterical with laughter. She had taken so many things for her itching and intestinal worms, but in the end, the Border Patrol and a fright proved to be the most effective remedy.

The Border Patrol Officers grabbed me before her. My hips turned out to be wider than the rolls of organza that I used as my hiding place. Somebody hollered to call the television station and the newspaper. The bust was a huge success for the Border Patrol. The television crews never came, and the newspaper article that was published was thin on details: "Raid in a garment factory." No one reported the fear that we felt, nor did they cover the humiliation of being treated like common criminals. They took us away in a bus with bars in the windows. I couldn't believe how, that very morning, I had walked those same streets as a free woman, and now I was a prisoner.

The drive was short. They brought us to a detention facility, and we stayed there for almost the entire day. Staying in one place for so long began to wreak havoc upon my body. My joints started to become stiff. This would happen to me whenever I sat for too long. This was the result of the rheumatoid arthritis that had settled in my body since I turned fifteen. From that day forth, my morning ritual has always been the same: I have to wake up an hour before getting out of bed and put the gears of my body into motion. First, my fingers, one by one; then my knees, moving them up and down; followed by my hips, lifting them up, then moving them to the left, shifting them to the right; followed by my wrists; and culminating with digital articulation. I sit up in bed slowly, like a robot that has just been activated. What for most other people seems like a very natural and involuntary movement, for me is a process of tendon and ligament stimulation before stepping one foot out of bed.

A tall and peevish-looking man with a tray full of stale sandwiches appeared in the room where they had us detained. I thought about tossing my ham-and-cheese into the garbage, but I ended up eating it.

It was a warm, starless night. They put us all back on the same bus with barred windows. Instead of taking Interstate 5 to Tijuana, the driver took I 10 to Mexicali. We had been on the road for two hours, and we were nearing Indio, when a dust devil clouded the bus-driver's vision. It was as if it had attached itself to the bus's fender. You couldn't see anything. I looked out the window and I began to see many overturned vehicles on the shoulder of the highway. I yelled at the top of my lungs: "Stop!"

The driver slammed on the brakes. A number of people fell forward from the impact. The bus-driver got off quickly. He must have seen something. Just a few inches away, a tracker-trailer had stopped with its lights off. If we hadn't stopped in time, many, if not all of us, would have died.

I felt as if I had been reborn. The pain in my joints had disappeared. I started to walk around inside the bus. Having prevented a catastrophe afforded me that privilege. I sat back down when I saw a young girl who was crying inconsolably. She was about fourteen years old. I tried to cheer her up: I promised her that I would not leave her alone and that I would take her with me to Tijuana.

Without ever having thanked me for saving his life, the driver of the bus showed us to a small, narrow passageway. It was the entrance into Mexicali. Upon passing through it, we had been officially deported.

A number of Mexican officials came to meet us. Finally, I thought to myself, someone to welcome us. But this reception was meant to interrogate us. Without the slightest trace of civility whatsoever, the Mexican officers escorted us to a door where we had to wait in line in order to be interviewed. The investigator's curtness was painful. I tried to complain: "Why are you treating us like this?" And as a punishment, he left me till the end.

Finally, after responding to numerous questions and convincing them that I was a Mexican citizen, a resident of Tijuana, Baja California, and a professional beautician, they allowed me to go free. I couldn't believe that the Mexican officers were actually worse than those in the United States.

The fourteen-year-old girl decided to come along with me after I promised to call her parents. It was nearly twelve o'clock at night. We walked a few blocks in search of the bus depot when we came across the door to a church. There were many people inside. They were observing the Easter Vigil. It was Holy Saturday, and Easter Sunday was just minutes away. We made the Sign of the Cross and thanked God for our having arrived safe and sound.

We left for Tijuana that very same evening. The moon shined upon the highway, La Rumorosa. My body became numb with cold. I covered the young girl with my sweater, and I swore never to return to the United States again. I had my career as a beautician. I would return to the beauty salon I left in search of all the dollars my brother promised. I didn't want to live any more with the uncertainty of whether or not the Border Patrol would come and arrest me, nor did I want to be forced to tolerate the jealousy of my fellow workers for doing the boss's hair and nails. In Tijuana, I wouldn't make much money, but I could be happy.

We reached my city on the following day. My intentions of staying lasted a week. My brother helped me to cross once again.

Rosa María
Bell, California

Get Me Down, Before I Slap You Silly!

When I reached Tijuana, I was so frightened that I wanted to go back to my beloved Mexico City, but my children wouldn't let me. They introduced me to a coyote. "This guy is going to take you across to the other side."

I brought along my niece, who was still a young lady. We set out on our own adventure at night. As we were about to jump over the chainlink fence that the gringos had put up against us, the coyote said, "Come on. I'll lift you onto the fence so that you can jump over to the other side." He left me hanging there. Then he yelled, "Come on, ma'am! Jump to the other side!"

I told him, "I can't!" And the more I tried, the less I could. It felt like my arms were being torn from their sockets, so I shouted over to the man: "Get me down before I get mad!" He didn't pay any attention to me until I told him, "If you don't get me down from here, I'm going to slap you silly!" So he brought me down, very upset.

"Well, if you can't jump across, then maybe your niece can," he said.

I told him: "If I can't jump over, then my niece can't jump over either."

"Oh, well, then I guess you're going to take the long way," he replied angrily then took us to another place where we could walk across.

On our way, we heard a whistling sound, so I asked my niece, "Did you hear that?"

"Yeah, it must be the Border Patrol."

"No. It's not the Border Patrol," I said. "If they were to see us, they'd arrest us. They wouldn't whistle at us."

After a long, scary hike, we made it across. From there, we started to run through the fields. We climbed up and down in the darkness. Since I couldn't run as well as my niece, I fell behind. I was afraid that I would step on some poisonous animal or that the Border Patrol would catch us. The anxiety was so intense that only those who have experienced it would understand. Finally, we ran into a very steep slope. There, my pants got caught on a tree trunk. I pulled and with the yanking, the trunk came loose and I was sent sprawling downhill along with the tree trunk, totally unable to stop. I fell flat on my face, all banged up and with a twisted ankle. I could barely walk, but with my niece's help, I was able to stand up. With a great deal of effort, I continued to walk. Every now and then, the coyote would tell us, "Hurry. Run. Hit the floor." That was our routine during that hare-brained adventure.

Eventually, we came to a place where there was a group of men. They stole the little we had and even tried to rape my niece. Thanks to the people who were with us, we were able to defend ourselves. We were very frightened, and I felt I couldn't walk anymore. My ankle was very swollen, but I had to keep on going. The coyote continued to yell at me, "Hurry up, ma'am!"

I told him that I couldn't, but he kept on insisting, "You're not hurt. Come on. Walk!"

There were spots where we could hear the sound of the cars. When we saw the lights from the helicopters, we hit the ground and ate dirt. There came a time when we had no water and nothing to eat. The men had taken everything from us. Our mouths were dry. We continued to run until we came to a place where we thought we were safe, but we discovered that we were surrounded by the Border Patrol. They arrested us and sent us back to Tijuana.

We didn't have anything: no money, nothing to eat, and no one to turn to. My niece and I took a walk, and we found shelter under a little tree. Once there, we embraced one another and started to cry over our misfortunes. Suddenly, the same coyote as before appeared before us. "Don't worry. We'll try crossing the border again tonight," he told us.

"I'm not crossing for anything in the world," I replied, but I changed my mind after I remembered my children. My love for my children was greater than any hardship, and it gave me the courage to give it another try.

We tried it again. And again, the Border Patrol caught us. This time, they detained us for almost four days. They released us, warning that if we tried to cross again, they were going to lock us up for a long time. We thought long and hard. Finally, we made our decision: we were going to give it one last try. We weren't going to let them catch us this time. It was all or nothing, and we were ready to put it all on the line. We took more precautions. Whenever we heard a car, we hid behind rocks and in the mud. We went on like that for two nights and a day. Without eating, without drinking water, and then, worst of all, an animal bit me. We didn't know what it was. I felt awful. I began to foam at the mouth. My body began to go numb. The last thing I remember is being carried to a car. My life flashed before me like a movie. I saw my mother in her coffin, dressed in white. I saw her son who was only a month old when she died. The complications from the delivery had been too much for her frail and malnourished body. My mother had left a newborn baby boy just one month old along with my other siblings: One was three; another, six; and I was four years old. There were five children left in my father's care. He was a field worker who suddenly found himself in a daily routine that included, on top of his work in the cornfields, running back home at noon in order to make sure his children had something to eat and then going back out into the fields again. Tired of exerting himself so much that year, he showed up one day with a woman: "Okay, kids. This lady here is going to be my wife, and she'll be a second mother to all of you. From this moment on, you're going to mind her and do everything that she tells you to. And I don't want to hear any complaining out of any of you." I was five-and-a-half at the time. Before long, my stepmother started to scold and beat us viciously, and she always put us to work around the house.

There was no water on the ranch where we lived, so we had to fetch it from a gully that was far from the house, and it was something we had to do every day. Since I was the oldest girl, my stepmother gave me the hardest chores to do, like grinding flour on the *metate* for dough as well as making tortillas three times a day. I was very afraid of her because when I didn't finish, she burned my hands on the frying pan. I woke up every day at one o'clock in the morning, and by the time the sun was up, I had already finished grinding and had made a pot of *atole* out of raw corn kernels. I also ground corn on the *metate*, and with that I made the *atole* and everything else. When she got out of bed, lunch was already made. In my spare time, my stepmother would send me to the gully to wash everyone's clothes. I did it without complaining, because if I said anything about her to my father, things only got worse for me. She had threatened all of us.

The worst was when my stepmother tried to sell me off to some man. I found out when I was eavesdropping on one of their conversations. She had already set a date with the man as well as the amount of money that she would receive for me. Because I had no one to go to, the only thing that came to my mind was to think about committing suicide; and since there was always rat poison in the house, I went and got some. I was just about to swallow it when my father arrived. As soon as he saw the poison, he ripped it out of my hands, and he was just about to hit me when he pulled up short. He forced me to tell him why I wanted to poison myself. I told him the truth: I told him about the years of mistreatment and abuse. He complained about it to my stepmother, then threw her out of the house. Papá acted very lovingly. After many months, my stepmother returned and asked for his forgiveness. He took her back, and the abuse and mistreatment started up again. I was now eight years old. Every once in a while, she would send us to school, only to pull us out because my brothers had to work in the fields and the girls in the house. She would send my little sister, the youngest one, to drop off lunch for Papá. My little brothers and I never knew what it meant to play. We had no childhood. It was nothing but work, work, work, all day long.

Due to a misunderstanding, one day they came and took my father prisoner. The same day that they took my father away, my stepmother beat him so hard for breaking a pewter spoon as he ate that he ran away from home. He was only seven years old. He lived down by the gully for eight days, the same amount of time that Papá was in jail. Once things were cleared up, they let him go free, and when he found out about what had happened to my brother, he gave that woman a good beating. He spent a whole day looking for my brother. It was already nighttime when he came across an old man who had seen a boy lying on a rock at the bottom of the gully. They found him nearly unconscious. As a result, my brother was never the same again. His whole body trembled. He could barely talk. Papá took him to a number of healers, but he never recovered completely.

My little sister, the youngest one out of all of us, was

perhaps the one who had it the worst. During the rainy season, there were always a lot of mosquitoes at the ranch, and every mosquito that bit us left a bump on our arms and our legs. I was able to take a bath by myself, but my stepmother washed my little sister. She was so cruel that she would rip off the scabs from her mosquito bites with a really rough washcloth. My little sister would bleed everywhere. She cried so torturously that one day my papá heard her. He gave my stepmother another good beating that day. But she wouldn't learn her lesson. She continued to treat us just as bad, if not worse.

One time, she hit my oldest brother and hung him from a tree. When she took him down, my brother ran to get away from her. So my stepmother threw a machete at him and hit him on the foot. My brother took refuge in an aunt's house, and they treated him there. As time went by, my brothers just wouldn't take it anymore: they fought with her continuously.

It's strange that the animal bite could bring me back to the day when one of my cousins tried to rape me. Luckily, some workers who were coming from the fields appeared on the scene. They defended me and took me to my house. That same cousin continued to stalk me. The car stops, but I don't see the faces of the paramedics carrying me into the hospital; the one who is looking at me is my uncle, my mother's only brother, whom I begged to take me to his house in Cuernavaca.

I also see the face of my first boyfriend, the moment when he asked me to marry him, my father's rage when he found out. My boyfriend's family was very wealthy, and they were said to be bullies. My father opposed the wedding, and every time that they would go to ask him for my hand in marriage, my father hid, and they could never find him. That's when my boyfriend's father spoke to me. He asked me to run away with his son. I told him that I couldn't do that because my father would kill us both.

A short time later, my boyfriend's mother became very ill, and on her deathbed she called for me. She made me swear to her that I would marry her son. On that day, I agreed to marry him. The wedding dress came from Mexico City. The animals that were going to be killed for the reception, which would last four to eight days as was customary in that town, had already been selected. They had picked the steers, the hogs, the turkeys, and the chickens.

In order to get married, I first had to escape from my house. The date had been set. On the day that I was supposed to run away, my uncle told my father about my plans. That night, my boyfriend showed up with an army of men on horseback, armed to their teeth. What he didn't know was that my father had had enough time to surround the house with armed men of his own in order to prevent me from leaving.

The time had come for me to go, but I remained inside. Time began to go by. The neighing of the horses could be heard outside. My boyfriend started to become impatient. His father came forward to find out what was going on. But before he reached the front door, he stopped at a tree, and there he was stung by a scorpion. My boyfriend immediately took him away so that the town doctor could see him.

On the following day, my boyfriend, very angry, came to see me, telling me that if I wasn't willing to go peacefully, he was going to take me by force. It scared me. Everything had become so complicated. On the one hand, my father's threats that he would rather kill my boyfriend than let me marry him. On the other hand, my boyfriend's threats that he would take me by force. I didn't know what to do. I didn't want to see either one of them get hurt. I loved my boyfriend very much, but I also loved my father. There was no way that I was going to allow them to hurt each other because of me. So I decided to say good-bye to my boyfriend forever. I asked my father to take me back to Cuernavaca. That night, an aunt who lived in Mexico City arrived, like an angel come down from heaven. I asked my father if I could go back with her. He agreed, saying that it would only be for a little while. We sneaked out under the cover of night. When I was in Mexico City, I missed my boyfriend terribly. I cried every night in silence. With the distance, I realized that I loved him more than life itself, but I stuck it out. At that time, another young man appeared in my life. I married him, and we had three children, two boys and a girl. We lived happily until the day when he got the crazy idea of moving to the United States. I did everything possible to get that idea out of his head. But it was useless. He left me alone with my children. At first, he sent money, but suddenly, I lost all contact with him. I had to get a job in order to provide for my children. Once they grew up, they decided to go look for him, and they found out that he had married another woman. They asked me to go with them to the United States. I said no at first. But my love for them was stronger than any of my fears or anxieties. Again, the fear of the Border Patrol, the hills, the ravines, and me at the brink of falling . . . I opened my eyes.

I had been unconscious for a number of hours, lost in the valley of memories. Looking very frightened, my children and my niece accompanied me in the hospital. They released me that same evening. Crying, my niece embraced me. Together, we had overcome all of the obstacles, and we weren't about to let anyone keep us out of the United States again.

Iginia
San Diego, California

He Sold Me to the Armenian

They hid me in the back of the van under one of the seats. Everyone had papers except me. They told me not to make a sound. I could hear everything: the conversation with the immigration officer, the inspection of the seats, the trembling of my body. I was paralyzed with fear. I had made the decision to exchange my land of *atole,* tamales, and *chilaquiles* for a nation of hamburgers and Taco Bell.

Leaving Mexico was for the best. "In the United States, people work hard, but they make a lot of money." I had heard it said so many times that, in the end, I decided to give it a try. I had nothing to lose; I had been living outside of my parents's house since I was sixteen. My mother's yelling had become intolerable. "You fucking lazy, good-for-nothing bum. Where do you think you can go to make something out of your life? Hey, bitch! I'm talking to you! You little shit, you're worthless!" My mother repeated those words to me so many times that they burned themselves into my memory, and they remain with me still, as if someone had tattooed them onto my body.

The Border Patrol officer didn't find me, and they allowed us to pass on through. I imagined the Puerto Rican's nervous hand putting the car into gear. His six-year-old son, another young boy, and a number of men were also traveling in the van. I was the only woman.

After a long drive, they removed me from my hiding place. I had expected to find a harsh, hostile environment, full of cliffs and precipices. It was exactly the opposite: there were flowers and vegetation all around. On one side of the road, there was a row of houses with big windows, all built exactly alike. But no one could be seen through the window. It was all so different than Tijuana, a disorganized city, and even more different than Mexico City, a tarnished city where there was something corrupt in all of us. Nor did it resemble Guadalajara, where I went without any money and not knowing a soul. Guadalajara is a city full of gardens and plazas, but where people are more concerned about the welfare of inanimate saints inside of a church than about those who are living outside of the church, begging for money to relieve their hunger.

The man from Puerto Rico was fifty years old. He was the boyfriend of a friend of mine in Tijuana. "This is your chance. My boyfriend is going to take people across tonight. Go for it," my friend suggested. He had told her that he was a single father. She explained to me that I could stay in his house for a little while, until I found some work. I agreed. I didn't have anywhere else to go.

His house was located in a remote area. The furniture was old, and there were four rooms that were completely empty. After only a few days, I realized that it was a house for coyotes. Carloads full of people would arrive each day. I waited on them. I soon realized that I had become the maid. I didn't complain because I felt as though it was my way to pay him back for helping me cross.

Everything changed one night when I felt the Puerto Rican's cold hands prying between my legs. My bedroom was a mattress tossed on the floor.

"Don't act like some kind of saint or something. You know you wanna fuck."

My heart began to beat against my temples. I tried to free myself from his sick embrace. We fought. A cold sweat ran down my spine. Mounted on top of me, he rubbed his limp penis under my hip. My heart was about to burst in my temples. I don't know where I gathered the strength, but I got up and pushed him onto the wall. The Puerto Rican fell to one side and growled like an animal. I tried to escape, but I slipped before reaching the door. I got back on my feet. He now stood before me. We stared at each other like two wild beasts set to scratch and claw and tear each other to pieces. All of a sudden, he seemed to grow smaller, his feet like claws firm in the ground. His breathing heavy, his fat gut covered in body hair. He looked at me with wanton eyes and an obscene smile. Just then, the sound of a siren could be heard. I turned to the window. I took advantage of the moment to leave the room. The door was unlocked. I tried to run outside, but the front door had a lock on it. He tried to catch up to me. I screamed, but no one came to my rescue. To my horror, I realized that everyone had left at night. The house was empty. I ran into a room with an armchair in the middle. He chased after me but couldn't catch me. It was a dangerous game of hunter and hunted. He couldn't catch me. Frustrated, he collapsed into the armchair. "Get outta here then."

I left running, and I didn't go back into the house until a car arrived. It was a fifty-five-year-old gringo. His name was Mr. Green. The Puerto Rican came out and ordered me to go back inside. He told me that on the following day I would go with Mr. Green because he didn't want me in his house anymore. I gathered up all my fears along with the two pieces of clothing that made up my whole wardrobe. It was a sleepless night, filled with anxiety. When Mr. Green woke up, I was already waiting for him next to the door. I got into his car, not knowing where he would take me. The bright, sunny morning made me feel more optimistic. During the drive, I discovered that Mr. Green was also a coyote. He spoke very little Spanish. I learned from him that the city where I had been living was called Chula Vista.

Mr. Green was a tall, hunched-over man. His eyes were very blue. His hair almost white. He told me that we were going to Santa Ana. An hour on the road had gone by, and I was frightened when he parked in front of a motel. There were two palm trees full of dates to one side of the motel, and it smelled of damp earth. A few minutes went by. My optimism didn't fade, sure that he was going to get separate rooms. Mr. Green was also tired. On the way, I noticed his sleepy face. He returned with only one key in hand. He escorted me up to the room, and I got scared when he entered the room with me. He calmed me down right away.

"*Yo no querer* nothing with you. You go *dormir. Yo dormir* on the floor. *Yo tú cuidar.*"

I lay down on the bed fully clothed, and he went to sleep on the floor. I was very scared. I fought not to fall asleep, but the fatigue and the sleeplessness of the previous night overwhelmed me. I woke up the following morning, and I found Mr. Green sound asleep. Unlike the Puerto Rican, the gringo had turned out to be a gentleman, or so I thought.

I was ready to continue the journey when Mr. Green took me to meet the hotel owner. He was a dark-skinned Armenian with no wrinkles. He scanned me from head to toe. The two took a few steps back. My breathing was suddenly cut short. They were making a deal over me. Mr. Green was selling me to the Armenian. I didn't know all of the details, but I understood enough to realize what was taking place. The whole situation upset me. I wanted to run away. I had never felt like an animal, to be bought and sold, to be traded and then completely forgotten.

Mr. Green left me with the Armenian, and I never saw

him again. I had no idea what this man was going to do with me. That very day, he took me to his house in the same city. His name was Mike. His house turned out to be a great, big mansion. He introduced me to his wife, his daughters, and his only son. In a short time, I came to understand the details of the operation: Mr. Green had sold me to the Armenian in perpetuity, and my salary would be $50 a week, with no days off.

The first week, when Mr. Mike notified me that he had opened a savings account in both of our names and that he would deposit my money there each week I realized that I would never see a single cent of the $50 that he promised me. I began to feel as though I really was a slave who deserved no better. My mother had told me so, so many times. "You lazy, good-for-nothing bum! You fucking dumb-ass, watch what you're doing!" That was the treatment that I received for as long as I can remember. In time, I came to understand that my mother verbally abused me and my brothers and sisters as a way to vent her own feelings due to the abuse that she received from my alcoholic father.

Many months went by, and I continued with my chores of cooking, ironing, cleaning the bathrooms, dusting the furniture, and attending to Mr. Mike's daughters. Something inside began to bother me. A vestige of dignity and of rage started to grow inside me to the point that I began to fight and argue with Mr. Mike's daughters, who treated me as if I really were a slave. One day I confronted him, and I told him to give me my money because I wanted to leave. He agreed. He took me to the bank that same afternoon. I remained in the car, sure that he would give me just over $1,000. Out of the corner of my eye, I saw him counting the money. He got into the car and handed it over to me. There was $100, all in $10 bills. I got very upset. I spit in his face and threw the money at him. Pale, he explained to me that the remainder went to pay off what he had given to Mr. Green for me. I swore at him as I got out of the car. He didn't try coming after me.

I walked through the streets of downtown Santa Ana. It was the first time that I had ever stepped foot outside of Mr. Mike's house. I didn't know where to go. I knew no one. The sirens on the police cars made me jump out of my skin. I thought that they could detain me. I figured they had the same authority as the Border Patrol. I didn't dare ask anyone for money. I was hungry, and I had wandered far from the civic center. I had walked for hours. I went back and sat on a bench close to a bus stop. I didn't want to give rise to any suspicions. As the afternoon gave way to nightfall, the city transformed itself before my very eyes. The luxury cars no longer drove around. Well-dressed people carrying briefcases disappeared, along with their employees with plastic bags in hand and a firm step.

As if they had stepped out of the steam rising from the sewage drains, vagabonds, prostitutes, and beggars began to emerge. I saw a different city before me. It reminded me of a neighborhood in Mexico City. The neon lights, the sound of the prostitutes's high heels as they crossed the street, the chatter of two drunks on the street corner. Everything started to happen as the night progressed. No one looked at me. It was as if I was invisible or as if I was so small that no one took notice of me. I felt a pain in the pit of my stomach.

A car pulled up to the curb beside me. From the window, a familiar face appeared. I was happy to see it. It was Mr. Mike's wife, who had been driving around looking for me. She took me back to the house. From slave I had been promoted to servant. Another year transpired, and I certainly would have stayed much longer had Mr. Mike not attempted to overstep his bounds with me. I was cleaning the bathroom when he came inside, and without closing the door, he dropped his pants and, very naturally, began to urinate in front of me. I was going to leave when he grabbed me by the arm. He tried to guide my hand toward his erect penis. I got scared and ran away, and I never went back.

While looking for work, I came across a Mexican family. They hired me to take care of their children. Two more years went by.

One morning, I woke with a tremendous desire to see my family. Four years had gone by, and I hadn't even written to them. They could have well thought that I was dead. I had the hidden hope that my mother would receive me with open arms. I saved up for a ticket and I decided to return to Mexico City.

"And where the hell have you gotten off to?" was what my mother said to welcome me.

I wanted to embrace her, tell her what had happened to me with Mr. Mike, with Mr. Green. But she hadn't changed. She was the same loathsome woman that I had left behind. Two weeks went by. I found the city to be more inhuman, corrupt, the streets chaotic. I had grown accustomed to the orderliness of the United States. I decided to return. I left the little I had with me, and I filled my backpack with candy that I bought at the market: candied pumpkins, *pipitorias*, *jamoncillos*, sweet potatoes, and marzipan. This would be my nourishment and my luggage.

I arrived in Tijuana, ready to cross on my own, without the help of any coyote. Exploring the edge of the border, I met a young Salvadoran man.

"Hey, you, I know the way. If you want, we can go across together." I accepted his offer.

We had our first setback before we even tried to cross. Two policemen arrested us. They accused my companion of kidnapping me, and they accused me of being a Colombian. I couldn't believe that this was happening to me in my own country. We realized that all they wanted was money. We gave them the money, and they let us go free. We picked a spot to cross. It was a question of waiting until the patrols had left. We made an improvised shelter next to some boards. The sky began to fill with storm clouds, and it started to pour. We were happy to see that the patrols had withdrawn. We jumped the fence and started to run. The mud made it difficult for us to move forward. The rain lasted for hours, but we continued to walk. We didn't stop until we reached a train station. It was two o'clock when we got there. We took the train to San Diego. We got off, and we realized that we had run out of money, and there was still a long way to go to get to Los Angeles. My companion decided that we should go back to walking after getting off on Las Pulgas Road, close to the freeway exit on the way to San Onofre. The downpour resumed. The cold began to filter its way in through our noses, through our mouths. It entered through every pore in our bodies. We had walked for eighteen miles. Our wet clothes made it more difficult to move. We were passing under a bridge when the young Salvadoran man collapsed. I thought that he had fallen in the mud. I went up to him and saw how pallid his face had become in contrast to his dark mustache. He was trembling. He told me to leave him there, that he was very cold, that his knee was hurting him. I held him and rubbed his chest. I took out the candy that I had brought from Mexico. And we started to eat it. I remember well what I said to him: "Are you going to give up? Real men never quit."

He looked at me with deep, sad eyes. "Look. I can't go on. Just go."

"What kind of man are you?" I shouted at him angrily.

He looked at me again. "Come on, then." It was hard for him to get back up. I saw that he really couldn't walk any further. I encouraged him to tell me about his homeland. He moved forward in silence. Neither one of us knew whether or not we had passed San Clemente yet. We spotted a place where two spheres, like a woman's breasts, could be seen. "San Onofre!" he said excitedly.

We went up to the place and asked the guard who was stationed there if we had already passed San Clemente. Without even answering us, he looked at us scornfully and hurried off. In just a few minutes, the Border Patrol had us surrounded.

"Run! Hide!" he screamed as he stood still.

I hid myself behind one of the poles. My companion did not move. I watched him from a short distance. He looked very bad. He couldn't stop coughing. I prayed to all of the martyrs and saints that they would not see me. I couldn't accept getting arrested after all the walking that we had done. All of our effort was going to be in vain.

Three patrol cars surrounded him. Meekly, he allowed himself to be taken. I had to make a decision: stay there until they had left, or give myself up and go with him. I chose the latter. They took us to San Clemente. We slept there until the following day. A bus came to pick us up along with some other detainees. The driver would not stop insulting us. When I was boarding the bus, my sweater fell. Before I could pick it up, he wiped his shoes on it. I felt so humiliated that I swore at him very angrily as I retrieved my sweater. His reaction was a threat. My disappointment grew when everyone else started to laugh at the incident, as if I was some kind of comedic sketch for their enjoyment. They dropped all of us off in Tijuana. I lost track of the young Salvadoran man. I tried to get a visa, but that was like daydreaming. I was denied. So I decided to cross without help from anybody.

With my experience from the first attempt, it was easier for me to get to San Diego. I didn't have any money, and I was hungry. This time, I ventured to ask for money. I got together enough money to buy a train ticket. I gathered up enough courage to buy a ticket to Los Angeles. I boarded the train, and I sat next to a young man who gave me the impression that he too was undocumented. We looked at each other briefly. I didn't move from my seat.

Time went by very slowly. A Border Patrol agent boarded at one of the stops. One by one, he went around asking people for their papers. As he stood in front of me, I found the courage I had lacked all along. The courage that I lacked to stand up to my mother's insults, the courage to confront my father for abandoning us, the courage to expose Mr. Mike. I gathered it all up and used it to look him straight in the eyes and say, "American citizen."

The young man sitting next to me did the same. We reached Los Angles at sundown.

María
San Diego

The Girl from Nicaragua Was Washed Away by the River

She couldn't have been more than twenty years old. Her beauty was calm, serene, though somewhat proud. She walked tall and erect, and her hands were very well kept. They were not the calloused hands of a woman who washes laundry and does all of the household chores. Her manner of dress caught my attention: a light pink sweater rested on her back, its sleeves tied around her neck in a delicate knot. She wore a pair of rose-colored pants, and her shoes were black with brown stitching. It was the only detail that didn't match her clothing. She was traveling with the group, but at the same time, she traveled alone. Not once did I hear her speak. She looked about her with a distant gaze.

She came from Nicaragua; I was from El Salvador. She was running away from something; I was fleeing the war, a war that caused everything to erupt, even the volcanoes. For her, to stay in Nicaragua must have meant something terrible; for me, staying in El Salvador meant continuing to bury the dead.

There were many of us who left El Salvador toward mid-June 1979. The bombings had destroyed all of our hometowns: Guazapa, Chalatenango, Morazán.

Only half of our family members had survived the massacres in Sumpul and Mazoto. War is a terrible, terrible thing. It washes away everything, like an overflowing river. It causes everything to explode. It destroys everything. That's war. You're afraid even to walk across the street because you worry that the soldiers will be waiting there just to shoot you: you not knowing who they are, them not knowing anything about you. A lot people ended up missing without anyone knowing why they had "disappeared."

In Guatemala, we were detained by a group of army reservists. They forced us off the bus. The girl from Nicaragua looked at them defiantly. Her pride prevailed. She emanated authority. They didn't ask her anything. Everyone re-boarded the bus, except for me. She looked at me without any expression in her eyes.

"This one stays," said the Guatemalan soldier. I was overcome with fear. I thought that they were going to make me "disappear." That's how they got rid of many people in El Salvador.

The driver intervened, "We're not moving from this spot until everyone is back on board."

The soldier looked at him for a moment. Then he looked at me. Then he looked at everyone else. "Go on," he grumbled.

We reached the border with Mexico at seven o'clock in the evening of that very same day. They kept everyone in a room. The room reeked of human excrement. There were urine stains everywhere. We barely fit. The girl from Nicaragua chose a corner, crossed her arms, and curled up into a ball. Her hairdo had been ruined. Her hair fell down over her shoulders. The heat was suffocating. Flies whizzed about the room, and clouds of mosquitoes swarmed down from the ceiling and buzzed around our heads. Two mice came shooting out from one of the corners of the room and ran impudently through the door. Two ladies screamed as soon as they saw them.

"Enough already! I can't believe you're making such a fuss over a pair of mice," the coyote exclaimed.

I went into the bathroom, and the foul odor penetrated my nostrils and even made me feel faint. They had us locked up in that room for twelve days, twelve days of retained excrement and intestinal pain. During that time, the girl from Nicaragua deteriorated a great deal. Her proud strut had disappeared. She moved slowly, as if dragging some heavy burden slung over her back. Her face had lost its luster, and her hair was a tangled mess. One night when I saw her shivering with cold, I offered her my wool sweater, and she took it. I could see how thin her face had become. She had lost a lot of weight. Dark rings appeared under her eyes. Her cheekbones had become more pronounced, and her sweater was missing a number of buttons.

"Everybody out!" The coyote gave his order, and we all left in silence. We took our seats. Our weariness was evident.

But our spirits were lifted once again on the road. The color had returned to the girl from Nicaragua. It appeared as if someone had pinched her cheeks. It was the first time that I had ever seen her smile. It was a big, familiar smile. I smiled back at her. I wanted to go up to her, but I didn't dare. I continued to admire her from afar. She carefully observed the road, which was full of trees and plants. We approached the river.

We stepped off the bus, and the coyote made us walk for a good stretch. "We're all going to cross the river! On the other side, we're going to walk to Oaxaca to avoid the Federal Police!" The order had been given. I was afraid to cross the river. During the rainy season in El Salvador, the rivers would overflow, and they would wash everything away. Just like the war, they would destroy the cornfields, the countryside, the livestock, and they would leave so many dead in their wake.

I looked around for her. She smiled at me again. I saw her approaching the riverbed. It seemed as though she wasn't afraid of the current at all. She tightened the straps of her shoes. Her petite feet sank into the mud, leaving an impression that was immediately erased by the water that flooded in from the river.

The coyote looked at the current with concern. "It's really coming down hard. Let's form a chain." He instructed us to hold hands. "Whatever you do, don't let go."

He grabbed a woman by the hand and plunged into the river. He advanced a few paces, and the current lifted him up like a tidal wave. We all got scared. He shouted: "Come on! Let's go!"

Trembling with fear, we submerged ourselves into the water. Our hands were shaking. The water was so cold. The current was too strong. It knocked us off balance.

"Just don't let go! Come on! Come on!"

The water came up to our waists. The girl from Nicaragua was one of the last ones in the chain. I was upset with myself for not staying with her. The coyote was just about to reach the other side. Many of us were still in the middle of the river, and a few were still close to the bank. We continued to push and pull with all our might. The human chain weakened with each passing moment. The coyote continued to yell: "Don't let go! We're almost there!"

Suddenly, the wind began to blow. A piercing howl came whistling through the trees. As we moved forward, the river itself became deeper. The water started to come up to our necks. A number of people screamed that they didn't know how to swim.

"No one let go!" the coyote continued to yell.

Without warning, we began to take a beating all over our bodies. The river brought rocks and brush along with it. The chain was broken. The girl from Nicaragua screamed helplessly. The current was too strong. She struggled to grasp onto one of the branches. We were petrified.

"Keep moving! Or we're all going to die!" the coyote shouted.

The girl continued to scream, her quivering hands battling the current. We all saw how she disappeared. Everyone reached the other side of the river, everyone but the girl from Nicaragua. We remained there for a short while. The women cried. The men walked along the riverbank to see if we could hear anything. The wind subsided. After a short time, the only thing we could find was her pink sweater, floating in the water.

That night I cried for the girl from Nicaragua. Lying down face up, in the middle of a cornfield, it seemed as though I could see her face in the most brilliant star. That night I dreamt that we had found her alive. I saw her come out from the trees. She stepped out from the cornfield, showered in light and wearing her melancholy smile. I spoke to her. A tug on the arm woke me up. "Stop talking so much. We can't get any sleep."

We walked for three days straight. It was nighttime. Our swollen feet refused to go on any longer. They took us to a rough spot of land. A bus came to pick us up in the morning in order to take us to Mexico City. We stayed there for six days before leaving for Nogales, Sonora. There were a lot of us. They packed us into two buses any way that they could. The first bus to leave was stopped unexpectedly by Mexican immigration officials, and they sent everyone back. I had better luck. No one stopped us along the way. We reached Nogales at the break of dawn. They put us up in some fleabag hotel and kept us there for three days.

Another coyote showed up, and they started taking us across one by one. In the end, there were just two men and three women remaining. They crossed us and found lodgings for us at a Motel 6. They rented a room, and we stayed there for another three days. Those were three days of hell, because two other coyotes joined us. While one of them kept his eye on me, the others raped the girls. They did this on various occasions. I thought about the girl from Nicaragua. Perhaps it was better that the river had washed her away.

When we left, the girls appeared to have aged ten years. They walked slowly, their legs pressed together, their heads bowed. They had changed. I thought about the girl from Nicaragua again. I cried almost all the way to Los Angeles.

José Luis
Huntington Park, California

God Made Us Disappear from the Border Patrol

"Down on the ground! Here comes the Border Patrol!" We ducked quickly under a withered tree. There were four of us women traveling together: one was sixteen, another nineteen, a sixty-year-old lady, and I was twenty-four. I pictured myself in handcuffs. We had nowhere to run. The Border Patrol was just a few steps away. The journey from Tegucigalpa, Honduras, to Tijuana and then the hop over to San Diego had been so long, and now it was all about to end.

A few moments went by when we began to hear some whispering. I didn't know what it was at first. It was coming from the older lady. She was praying the Hail Mary. The coyote became infuriated. He demanded for her to keep quiet. "Shut up. You're going to give us away," he said, gnashing his teeth and raising a fist up to her face.

She had her eyes closed and continued to pray: "Hail Mary, full of grace, the Lord is with you. Blessed are you among women, and blessed is the fruit of your womb, Jesus . . ."

The coyote became even more enraged because the two young girls and I started to pray as well: "Holy Mary, Mother of God, pray for us sinners, now and at the time of our . . ."

"Shut up! Shut up!" the coyote insisted.

"Hail Mary, full of grace, the Lord is with you . . ."

The horse's trot could be heard drawing closer and closer. We watched as the officer dismounted from his horse. He came toward us, and with a flashlight, he lit up our hiding place. He had caught us. There was a silence. About two minutes went by. We didn't move. Inexplicably, the officer turned around and rode away on his horse. It was as if he hadn't seen anything.

"It's a miracle! God made us disappear from the Border Patrol!" the older lady said.

It was a sign for us to continue. We walked for many hours. We were going in circles. After seeing the same places again, we asked the coyote if he was lost. He told us he was, but if we were able to get across a nearby lagoon, we would be just fine.

A moonless night had fallen. It was pitch black. It was difficult for us to make out the lagoon. He assured us that it wasn't very deep, that it would only come up to our waists at the most.

"I'll go first. You should go last so that you can help the chubby, older lady," I told him.

The coyote agreed, and I began to walk. But the more I walked, the deeper I sank. Halfway across, I realized that it wasn't a lagoon: it was a swamp. I was stuck in the mud. One more step and I would have sunk to the bottom. "Watch out! It's a swamp!" I was able to yell.

I made it back to the surface as best as I could. I was disoriented. I didn't know whether to go back or to keep moving forward. The fear of death paralyzed me. I decided to move ahead, and I was able to reach the other side. I crawled up to a tree. From the other side, the coyote instructed me to break off a big branch in order to help the others make it across, and that's what I did. I don't know where I gathered the strength to drag the others across the swamp one by one. But as soon as everyone was on safe ground, I began to cry uncontrollably. I realized how close I had come to dying. We were drenched in mud and shivering with cold. It was five in the morning. We walked for a short while until we reached our scheduled meeting place. There was a car waiting for us. And like enchiladas, they stuffed us in the trunk of a large automobile. That's how we made it to Los Angeles.

Leyla
Winneteka, California

We Were Short 1,400 Quetzals

After counting all of the money, we realized that we were short 1,400 quetzals. We were not scared, because we were innocent. But in the midst of a civil war, even the innocent are guilty. Corpses appear on street corners. Their murderers go about freely, and no one dares to turn them in. We would be no exception. The victims's families recognize those responsible, but they head for the hills before ever confronting them. To be indigenous in Guatemala is to be suspected of belonging to a guerrilla organization. Neither Juan nor I were members of any guerrilla faction; we were members of a co-op that had come up 1,400 quetzals short, and neither one of us knew who might have taken the money. The warning came that very afternoon.

"Look, if you guys don't leave today, they're going to kill you," a friend told us.

"Ah, c'mon. How would you know, anyway?"

"Because they've already hired the hit men to kill you."

"But why us?"

"Because they can."

I wanted to take my wife with me. We were expecting the birth of our first child. "You go, Pascual. I'd just slow you down," she said.

"Come with me. If you stay here, they'll kill you."

Juan arranged for our departure from Guatemala. It was very hard to leave our homeland behind. Even more so in a time when the landowners would keep all of our possessions. My wife was very upset. I could see how she said good-bye to everything with her eyes. She bid farewell to the mountains, to the lakes, to the cornfields, to the grass, to the reeds, to Cuchumatán, to Uspantán, and to the city of Tres Cruces. We walked for a long time, so long that I can't even remember how many days had gone by. She nearly died on me in Oaxaca. She would throw up everything that she ate. She didn't want to go on any farther. She would rather die there. I forced her to drink a bottle of juice each day. With help from Juan, we were able to reach Mexico City by bus, from there to Chihuahua, and from Chihuahua to Ciudad Juárez.

In Ciudad Juárez, my wife got very sick from the cold. Snow, like a mantel, had covered the entire city. I decided to take her to a place that was warmer. With the little money that I had left, we headed for Culiacán. Once there, we rented a hotel room, and on the following day, we looked for work. There was work to be found, but not a house or any place where we could stay. Nor was there any potable water. People washed and bathed in the canals. Worst of all, pigs bathed in the very same canals, and that same water was used for drinking. In Guatemala, there was war, cruelty, and intolerance, but in Mexico, there was poverty, sickness, and little hope.

"Man, your wife ain't lookin' so good," Juan informed me.

"I know. But you know that we can't stay here."

"You want to go all the way to the United States?"

The gunmen were going to kill us back in Guatemala, but hunger would kill us here.

"Yeah, let's go."

We went to Mazatlán, and from there we headed for Tijuana. We found a coyote in front of the cathedral. That same night, we attempted to cross the border by passing through La Colonia Libertad. We were going to cross by crawling through some tunnels. My wife looked weaker and weaker.

"You need to hang on just a little bit longer."

"I feel really bad, Pascual," she said.

She looked so thin. Her breasts had disappeared. Only her belly appeared to be getting bigger and bigger all the time.

The coyote directed us to some tunnel. "You're going to pass through here," he said.

So that no one would get lost, he told us to grab hold of the hem of the pants leg of another person, forming a human chain. We began to crawl through the tunnel on all fours. As we moved forward, it felt as if we were stepping on top of something. There were people lying down and others half sitting. We didn't know if they were dead or alive. It was a cold, dark place. We finally reached the other side. A car was there waiting for us, and it took us to National City. That afternoon, the coyote said, "Get the women ready. They're going first. The Border Patrol doesn't bother with them when going through San Clemente. The men will leave later."

I got up from where I had been sitting and said, "What do you take us for? Fools? I don't think so. Let me know right now if you're going to cross us all at the same time or not. I'm not going to leave my wife in the state that she's in."

"If you don't want to be separated from your wife, you'll have to be patient. I'll try to cross you together," he said, lowering his voice.

We arrived in Los Angeles on the afternoon of January 28, 1981. By December 1983, my son was already a little boy. I had a job: I was operating a pushcart, but I was operating it without a license. One day, the police stopped me and took me to jail. On our trial date, they treated us as if we were dangerous criminals. There were twenty of us, all in a row, bound by a single chain. Each of us was shackled at the waist, the hands, and the ankles. The judge set us free, but the Border Patrol was there waiting for us as soon as we left the courthouse. They deported us to Mexicali. From Mexicali, I went to Tijuana to cross back over again. My wife and child were waiting for me.

It was very easy to find someone to take me across. We left the same night that I arrived in Tijuana. It was terribly cold. Around two in the morning, I started to shiver, and my teeth began to chatter. I felt something was happening to me. "I'm going to freeze to death," I thought to myself. I went up to the coyote and told him, "I'm freezing to death. I can't take it anymore. Please, let me get some heat from your body so that I can hold out." I looked so miserable that he gathered a bunch of trash around me and held me in his arms. We were like that for quite a while. Then, I'm not sure if I fainted or fell asleep. We crossed into San Isidro, California, at three o'clock in the afternoon. While we were walking, I was very surprised to see women's underwear strewn about everywhere. We came to a small mountain where some men where charging people for the right to cross the river. I asked the coyote what that was about. He explained to me that we should just pay them off because that way they would protect us from the thieves. Otherwise, they themselves would "shake us down" for everything we had, including our clothes. "Around here," he told me, "if it's not the coyotes then it's the thugs; or if not them, then it's the *pollos* themselves. This is no man's land. Not even the police or the Border Patrol dare come down here."

We crossed at midnight. We walked until we reached the freeway, where we sprinted across. A car was waiting for us there. During the drive, I stared at the highway and thought about some girls who told me how Mexican immigration officers had taken them to a hotel. One of them told me how she allowed herself to be seduced by them so that she would be able to cross without any problems. It took us a day to reach Los Angeles, where my wife and child were waiting for me.

Pedro
Los Angeles, California

The Shot Hit Right Next to Me

I had hoped to finish my degree, but the war prevented me from doing so. If a person didn't support the government, then he must have been a guerrilla sympathizer. Neutrality was an impossibility. I was one of the half million people who fled the violence in El Salvador.

On the day of my scheduled departure, I woke up very early. I embraced my father as I bid him farewell. He hid his face as he hugged me; he didn't want me to see him cry. I knew that our parting was breaking his heart, but he understood that it was best for me to leave the country as soon as possible.

A childhood friend accompanied me on the adventure. We left with $300 in our pockets and a great deal of confidence that we would make it to the United States any way that we could. All that we knew for certain was that we would have to cross through Mexico, get to Tijuana, pass into San Diego, and not stop until we reached Los Angeles. My mother and my brother were waiting for us there.

I was twenty and Tony was eighteen. It was the first time we had ever been outside of El Salvador. We arrived at the airport. We sat down and waited for our plane to leave. We made a pact that—come what may—we would not turn back. We began to engage in meaningless chatter, when suddenly, as if we had planned it together, we both started to cry. I wanted to give him a hug; perhaps he was thinking the same thing, but we had both been taught that men do not hug each other, nor do they cry in public. We dried our tears in silence.

In Guatemala, we were preparing ourselves to board a bus to Mexico when a man approached us. I realized that he had been watching us for some time now. We were very wary of him at first, but after a while, we grew to trust him. We told him about our plans to go to the United States. He asked our ages. When we told him how old we were, we could see clearly that he was on the brink of tears.

"You're the same age as my two sons. Did you know that? I want to help you."

He gave us an address in Mexico City along with the name of an attorney. He told us to tell him that we were his nephews. We boarded the bus, happy that we now had somewhere to go in Mexico.

The border with Mexico was only a short distance away when seven men climbed onto our bus. They started to demand money and jewelry. I could not believe my own eyes. The shock left me speechless, but it passed when the leader of the gang fired a shot right next to me. The blast left me momentarily deaf. Metal fragments fell onto my pants. Nervously, I handed him two quetzals. Tony gave him the ring and the necklace that his mother had hung around his neck the day that we departed. We thought that the scare was over. We never imagined that a bigger one was yet to come.

At the Mexican border, another kind of assailant appeared on the scene; these wore insignia and government uniforms. They boarded our bus. They took everyone who had a Guatemalan passport off the bus and escorted us to a room. There, they threatened to send us back if we did not provide them with a certain amount of money. Thanks to the intervention of a few public officials who were traveling with us on the bus, we were saved. They also helped us with two subsequent customs inspections before reaching Mexico City.

The attempted assaults upon us continued in Mexico City. Another group of men stepped on board. They said that they were Mexican immigration officers, and they told us that we had to prove that we were Mexican citizens; otherwise, they would have to send us back to Guatemala. They arrested a number of people, but Tony and I were able to get away. We reached the Mexican capital at eleven o'clock at night. We decided to rent a room in a motel that didn't look so bad from the outside. But there was a chilly surprise waiting for us in the room, because we had never stayed in a motel before. We came across something in the bathroom that we had never seen before. There were two knobs on the shower. We didn't know that one was for the hot water and the other was for the cold. As a result, I took a shower in freezing cold water. It felt as if ice was being poured down my spine and a frozen mist was falling from the showerhead. After I finished, I warned my friend about how cold the water was. When he stepped out of the shower, I could see some kind of vapor emanating from his pores. He made the same comment that I did: "Hey, can you believe how cold the water is here?"

After taking our cold showers, we went out into the street to take a look around, and we laughed when we saw how red our faces were. I wanted to see the Palacio de Bellas Artes. We met some girls there who took us on the metro to the zoo in Chapultepec. They made us feel very welcome with their hospitality and amiable nature. That same day, we went to go see the friend of our "uncle." We explained to him that we wanted to fly to Tijuana. He called the airline. He told them that we were his relatives and that we were going as tourists. He asked us for the money that we needed to purchase the tickets. In order to protect ourselves, we had hidden our money inside our down jackets. We had unsown the insides and stuffed the money in through a slit. The bills had shifted around everywhere inside. We were forced to dismantle our jackets completely in order to remove the money. There were feathers everywhere, and the attorney's office was suddenly full of feathers. We were quite embarrassed. We told him that we were sorry, but our laughter gave us away.

That same day our new friend transferred us to a hotel. He burst out laughing when we told him about our cold showers. Then he explained how to use the faucet handles. On the following day, one of the attorney's employees came to pick us up. He drove us to the airport. Once seated on the plane, I started to play with all of the buttons. Moving my seat back and forth, I was reading the instructions when Tony said, very annoyed, "Hey, man, cool it. People are going to think that this is the first time we've ever been on an airplane." We both started cracking up.

We got excited when touching down in Tijuana. We were very close to our final destination, or so we thought. After deboarding the plane, we had to pass through two customs inspections and then go to a waiting room where they asked the passengers their nationality. They separated the Mexicans from the others. About seventy people who had claimed not to be Mexican citizens were put to one side. Approximately fifteen immigration officers surrounded us and formed a circle; from there, people left one by one to a little room where—we were informed—they were taking every last cent of the people's money. In my anxiety and despair, I searched my mind: if I just ran out of that circle, they couldn't chase after me and leave all of those people behind.

With no time to lose, I took off running. They started to yell at me to come back. Tony, after seeing me, took off running, too. We ran first, then slowed to a walk. We were already nearing the exit when another couple of officers got in our way. To our relief, all they wanted to do was to check our luggage. We took a taxi to El Económico Hotel in Tijuana. We went shopping. We needed to look like "tourists," we had been told this was the thing to do.

We were approached in the street by a coyote who recognized our "touristy" appearance. We agreed upon a price to cross the border, and he said he would come for us in the morning.

He picked us up at four o'clock in the morning. We came to a fence that we slipped through easily. We went up and down a very small mountain where we stayed for a short while. We heard footsteps nearby. The coyote told us that it was another *pollo*. The young man eventually went by, without ever noticing us. He was crossing all alone. We were able to reach the train station. We boarded very calmly when two immigration officers stepped on and asked everyone for their papers. Upon seeing this, our guide took off running. We were arrested by the Border Patrol. They sent us back to Tijuana. We had hardly taken a few steps into Tijuana when another guide approached us. He promised to get us across the border. On the following day, we waited for the Border Patrol guards to change shifts. Our guide gave us the sign and we started to run. The officers shouted for us to stop. But we just ran faster. They didn't follow us. We crossed the line. A pickup truck was waiting for us farther up the road. There were already about fifteen people inside. We were packed like sardines. They covered us with an enormous rug. We looked like some kind of bundle of cargo. We thanked God that it was wintertime, because if not, we would have dehydrated. Once we passed through the San Clemente checkpoint, they allowed us to sit up. The first thing I saw was the sea gulls. It filled me with joy to see them flying around freely. Our first stop was in Santa Ana, where they began to call our families. They drove Tony and me to East LA. That's where I first heard the word "burrito." The coyote asked me if I wanted to eat a burrito (flour tortilla taco). "Sure," I said, "if donkey meat is the kind of meat you all are used to eating around here, then we'll have to give it a try." It tasted really good.

My brother arrived an hour later. He paid the respective "customs fees," and they allowed Tony and me to go free.

For quite a long time, I judged an entire country based on a few "bad apples" that I had come across on my journey. It wasn't until I met a family from Michoacan that I learned not to condemn a whole nation because of a few bad Mexicans. I have very fond memories of everyone who helped us along the way.

Vladimir
Los Angeles, California

My Cousins Came over from California

I was barely twenty years old and already thinking about killing myself. I hated my life. I felt empty inside, worthless in every sense of the word. I figured that suicide was the best way to put an end to my miserable existence. I asked myself if there was anything that could inspire me to go on living, or if there was anything that could give me the courage to put an end to it once and for all. I felt as though I were dying a little bit each day.

My mother came to see me. She asked me if I would like to go to the United States. Some distant cousins had come over from California, and I could live with them once I got to Los Angeles. I put off the idea of taking my own life. I decided that I was going to do something for her before "sacrificing myself." I still don't know if my mother was the motive or the pretext for my journey to the United States. Maybe the real reason was to hide from myself, from the cowardice of not being able to take my own life.

In Tijuana, my cousin put herself in charge of finding and contracting a coyote. We crossed that same night. We had to run, duck, throw ourselves on the ground, retreat, then take off running again. My pulse was racing a mile a minute with fear, and it felt as though my heart was caught between my ears because the beating was so loud. It was the first time that I had ever run away and hid myself from someone as if I was some kind of criminal. I was afraid of bumping into a tree or one of the horses ridden by the Border Patrol agents around there. Nevertheless, I had to run blindly or I would be left behind. I felt stupid running in complete darkness, in an unfamiliar place.

An ugly, fat man was waiting for us in San Clemente. He led us to a car parked in a dark, secluded place. He told me to sit in the front seat. We waited for a girl from Sinaloa who was pulling up the rear. I thought that maybe those two guys would do something to us. They were strange and vulgar men. The fat one talked very dirty to my cousin and the other girl, but he was respectful to me.

On the way to Los Angeles, the two men began to argue. They spoke pure nonsense. We reached South Gate. I wanted to get out in a parking lot, but the fat guy's partner told me to stay in the car. The fat guy intervened. He told the other one to let me be because I had already paid, and it was true. They took my cousin and the other girl because they didn't have any money to pay the coyotes. My cousin had spent all of her money in the discotheques before we left. I tried to convince them to let her go free by giving them all the money I had left, but they refused.

My cousin later told me that the coyote had raped her, and blamed me for this. I went to live with another cousin, where I was forced to meet my fate. I arrived during the winter, and on many nights, it was too cold for me to sleep. I went hungry; I was humiliated; they even locked me up; and the insults were a daily occurrence.

I don't love my cousins, but I don't hate them, either. Now I'm just completely indifferent.

Elsa
Los Angeles, California

After All I Had Done for Him . . . and He Betrayed Me

He was the most handsome young man that I had ever seen. He had a cleft chin and a lock of straight hair that fell over his forehead. His eyebrows wrinkled when he spoke. And his laugh was loud. He didn't smile; he laughed, and his howls of laughter could be heard throughout the store.

I worked as a cashier, and he was the salesman on the floor. On our first day working together, I gave him a ride home. On the way, we spoke as if we had always known each other. When we reached his house, he got out, and we continued to talk through the car window, him bearing down upon me, with arms folded. When we said good-bye, he leaned his head forward and kissed me on the mouth. I dreamt about him all night.

After knowing him for only two weeks, I knew that I wanted to spend the rest of my life with him. He couldn't take his eyes off of me while we were at work.

"Leave your parents and come live with me."

"Uh-huh, but don't you think it would be better if we got married first?"

"Let's get married then."

My parents had a problem accepting this. They were

alarmed at our rush to get married. Two days before our wedding day, he showed up at the store in an awful state. His hair was a mess. The smell of beer was oozing from his pores. He hid his eyes behind a pair of dark sunglasses.

"What happened to you?"

"You know, the bachelor party."

After we were married, we rented a very small apartment. We had the bare necessities. I didn't need anything more. I had him. Each Sunday, I lit a candle to the Blessed Sacrament so that my happiness would never end. At the store, he continued to be the gentle and affectionate man that I had known. In the evenings, we would take long walks. He liked to sneak into the alleys. He drowned me in his kisses, and we would leave laughing hysterically.

My parents were concerned about our financial situation. My car had broken down, and we didn't have enough money to fix it. After three months, my happiness grew greater: I was pregnant. I wanted a boy who would have his eyes, his straight black hair, with the lock that would fall over his forehead. Although were happy, my parents showed concern.

"Well, you can't work anymore."

"I'm pregnant. Not crippled."

"No. It's better if you just stay home."

"Uh-huh, but can't I work?"

"No. I'll find another job."

"Uh-huh. Whatever you say."

My visits to the Blessed Sacrament became more frequent. I prayed that my baby would be born healthy. Friction between my husband and my parents started due to our lack of money and the concern about the future of our child.

The first time that he came home late, he reeked of beer and had a very cold look on his face.

"Where were you?"

"Why do you want to know?"

"Because I'm your wife."

"My wife who's getting really fat."

That night, I cried until dawn. I didn't notice when he left for work. The situation grew tense. Problems started coming in through the front door, the roof, the cracks in the walls, and the door hinges. My delivery date was only a week away when he told me he planned to go to the United States.

"You're going to go to the United States when I'm about to give birth to your baby?"

"Your family won't let us be happy."

"You can't leave me right now!" I told him, drowning in my tears. "How are you going to leave Ecuador if you don't have a passport?"

"One of my buddies knows how to get across without any problems."

"You're crazy! You can't leave. At least stay until your baby's born!"

"There's no time. We're leaving tomorrow."

I felt as though someone had pulled me up by the hair and dropped me from an unsuspected height. The man who was my everything was leaving, and I could do nothing to stop him. Crying, I wrapped my arms around his neck. I loved him so much. I felt like I was going to die from nostalgia.

I packed our smallest suitcase for him. He told me to pack only two changes of clothing. He couldn't take any more than that. My family was furious with him.

"How could he leave you right when you're about to give birth?"

"Mom, it's just that his friend is offering to take him across for free. He has to take advantage of the opportunity."

"A responsible man wouldn't do that."

"His mind's made up."

"Don't worry. You can come live with us for as long as you want."

"Thanks, Mom."

That night, we hugged each other as we strolled down the same streets where we walked when we were dating. I began to tremble with anxiety. He held me. My world was falling to pieces all around me. We kissed. I tried to change his mind one more time.

"Have you really thought this through completely?"

"Yes. I've already thought about it, and my mind is made up."

"And what if something happens to you?"

"You'll have my baby."

His reply made me furious. "You don't care about our baby! You don't care about anything anymore! All you care about is leaving. Now I'm fat. Now I'm ugly. You just want to leave me. Admit it!" We had reached the apartment.

"Think whatever you want," he told me angrily.

I confronted him inside the house. He was seated in the wicker chair, his head buried in his hands. I wanted to run my fingers through his black hair. Kiss the curve of his ears. Brush his neck with my tongue. "If you don't want to stay, then go."

He left in the morning without saying good-bye. He had left his suitcase at the door. I moved in with my parents that same day. All of the anxiety accelerated my labor. I gave birth to a baby boy with black hair without complications. I cried the first time that I watched him suck hard on my nipple. His tiny hands held my breast.

A letter arrived four weeks later. It came accompanied by a money order for $150.

Magdalena,

Crossing the border wasn't easy. I found a job. I'll call you soon. How's my boy? Or was it a girl?

Efraín

I cried with joy. I read the letter over and over again. I looked between the lines for those loving words that I needed so much to hear. I learned it by heart. Other letters followed, coming more and more sporadically.

Cristian, our son, had turned a year old, and he still did not know his father.

"Forget about that man. He's never coming back for you."

"Efraín hasn't forgotten about me, Mom," I said, crying.

"You'd do well just to forget him. He hasn't even taken the time to come and see his own son."

"How can he leave the country without any papers?" I was ashamed of myself for attempting to justify the unjustifiable. In no letter had he even asked for a photograph. I was the one who gave him detailed accounts about how our son was doing: the first time he said "Pa," the time he fell and busted open his forehead. "Blessed Sacrament, please don't let him forget about me!" I prayed every night. "Make him want to see his son!" I became a religious devotee. I went to church every evening. My mother took care of Cristian because I had returned to the store to work as a cashier. I filled my days with other concerns to keep my mind off of him, but at night I cried from missing him so.

I was eating breakfast when the phone rang. His voice was the same: "Magdalena, come with me."

"Efraín? It's Efraín!" I yelled out to everyone else.

"A man is going to come by for you."

"But I can't leave Cristian. He's too young."

"I miss you so much."

"I miss you, too."

"How's my boy?"

"He's looking more and more like you every day."

"Then he must be really handsome." We burst out laughing.

I forgave him for not writing over the last few months.

"Do you remember our little strolls?"

"How could I forget: you gave me a baby on one of them." We started laughing again. There was a pause. Voices could be heard in the background.

"Who's there with you?"

"Just some friends," he answered, annoyed.

"Uh-huh. Guy friends or girl friends?"

"I told you, just friends," his voice turned harsh and he asked, "Do you still love me?"

"I adore you!" I replied.

"Then come with me to Los Angeles."

We agreed that a woman with a child would pass by for me, and she would take me to where he was staying. My parents tried to convince me to stay.

"This is madness!" my mother said.

"Have you forgotten that you have a child to think of?" argued my father.

"You're willing to abandon him to go with that man?" added my older brother.

I didn't listen to them. All I knew was that I would soon be by his side. My father warned me that if I left, things would not be the same with them. From that day on, my mother did nothing but cry. We worried about her health. The pain and anger provoked by my leaving was so great that they practically stopped talking to me. In a second phone call, Efraín gave me the precise instructions for my trip.

On the day of my departure, I decided to cut my hair and leave it loose. I wanted to look younger. I carefully chose the clothes that I was going to wear. I decided on black dress slacks and a blue blouse with a jacket that matched, and I wrapped a black silk scarf around my neck. I also wore the black overcoat that went down to my ankles. I kissed my baby in his bed, telling him that I would come back with his father.

The woman who came by looking for me looked safe. She was punctual when picking me up. I thought about my son and his father. About how much I had missed him. I smiled to think that I would soon see him again.

~ ~ ~

The plane landed at six-thirty in the afternoon, Mexico City time. I experienced my first humiliation when an immigration officer searched me completely. The lady explained that because Ecuador shares a border with Columbia, all of us Ecuadorians are suspected of being drug smugglers. We stayed in the Hotel Casa Blanca in the heart of the city. On the following day, the woman, her nephew, and I boarded a DC-10 jumbo jet destined for Tijuana. They served us a meal on the flight. It was the first time I had ever tried Mexican food. I was greatly surprised when I saw how small the airport was in comparison to the one in Mexico City. They had told me that Tijuana was one of the most frequented cities in the world. Efraín had explained to me that I would have to pass as a Mexican from Guadalajara. Without much difficulty, I convinced the immigration official in Tijuana that I was from Guadalajara. He let me go without any problems. A man was waiting for us outside of the airport. He was the father of the boy that the woman had brought with her. He took us out to eat, but I lost my appetite when they informed me that they were going to leave me all by myself in that city that was so foreign to me. They would go across the line that same evening. They had the documents to do so. They took me to the Hotel El Cacho. They said good-bye, and they told me not to open the door for anyone until a woman called "La Nana" came. She showed up that same evening. I hugged her as soon as I saw her and started to cry. The woman, advanced in years, put my hands together and asked me to stay calm and tranquil, and she told me to pray to God that I would be reunited with the father of my child that evening. Then she asked for all of my belongings. I gave her my earrings, watch, rings, and bracelet, everything made of gold. She promised that she would return them to me. She also took all of the money I had. She only left me with $10. She assured me that two men would come for me in a few hours and that they would take me across the border.

Two hours went by, then four, then five and six. No one came by. I couldn't do anything but cry. Night came, and nobody came to my door. I was so tired and so scared that I didn't realize exactly when I fell asleep. When I woke up, it was daytime. I looked at myself in the mirror. My eyes had turned into two *empanadas* because they were so swollen from crying so much. An entire day went by. I bathed in water that seemed to have come from the refrigerator. There was no hot water. The hotel owner sold me some milk and bread. At around noon on the third day, two men appeared at my door. They came on behalf of La Nana. Their instructions were concrete: "Just follow us. Don't talk to us unless it's absolutely necessary. And don't talk to anybody else either."

We went across the city to the coyote's house. I spoke very little along the way. They noticed that I used the word *ya* a lot, and they told me not to.

The coyote's house turned out to be located in a very poor neighborhood. There were eight men inside, all guides, according to what they told me. There was a total of fifteen people, in addition to one of the coyote's sons. We all had to share one bathroom.

Among those who were going to cross the border was a man from Columbia with very dark complexion. The coyote told him that it was going to be harder for him because of the color of his skin.

I slept in the coyote's wife's bed. I was awakened in the middle of the night by some shouting. The coyote and his assistants had gotten drunk. The coyote started yelling at his wife, saying that she had cheated on him. They ordered us to go back to bed. I saw how the man approached her, intent on hitting her. The rest of the group and I prevented him from doing so. The man swore at all of us. He was furious. He finally fell asleep, and we were able to rest until the morning. On the following day, the woman prepared a couple of dishes called *caldo de res* and *carne asada*. That was the second time in a week that I enjoyed Mexican cuisine at its very best. The coyote warned us that we needed to eat very well. Had I known what awaited me, I would have treated it as though it was my last meal.

The coyote's house was a few blocks away from the chainlink fence that marks the border. We hopped the fence without any difficulty. Once on the other side, the coyote explained to us that, if the Border Patrol were to catch us, we should say that we were Mexicans, and we should never, for any reason whatsoever, provide them with our real names.

We started to walk. A number of the coyote's assistants came with us. Two men accompanied me, because I was under social protection. We started our descent into "The Valley of the Fallen." I called it that because there were a lot of holes. We started to walk, and to walk uphill. The sky was filled with helicopters that the guides called "mosquitoes." We walked for a stretch, and then we threw ourselves on the ground. Just like that, they ordered over and over again, "Run! Run!"

I yelled, "I can't!"

One of the men pulled on one of my arms, and the other one took the other arm. "Run! Hit the dirt! Run! Hit the dirt! The helicopters are right on top of us."

It was worse than in a jungle. All of that subsided once we reached a gigantic tree. We all regrouped there, since we had been separated into smaller groups along the way. We started running again in a single-file line. Then, all of a sudden, the coyote yelled, "We made it!"

Before we could catch our breath, they ordered us to hide in some bushes. The Border Patrol could be seen just a few yards away. We all dropped to the ground. There was excrement everywhere. I wanted to puke. Insects flew around in swarms over the filth. We stayed there until the Border Patrol had left. One by one, we crossed over the train tracks. We cut across the backyard of a house and walked out onto the street. The coyote took me by the hand, and said, "Let's walk together like boyfriend and girlfriend."

He put his arm around my waist. We walked slowly as we pretended to talk. He led me to a pickup that turned out to be quite peculiar. The back part was made like an empty metal box. The opening was where the driver and the other two passengers sat. About six people could fit in there. They put me behind the seat. I was beginning to doze off when the pickup stopped, and they moved me up to the front seat, where the coyote and La Nana were seated. We continued on to a place called San Onofre. They had a mobile home there. It was around three o'clock in the morning when we arrived.

My heart skipped a beat from the excitement of knowing that very soon I would be able to see Efraín once again. They changed cars at the mobile home. Since I was the only woman, they decided to go drop me off first. I will never forget the names of the streets that they took so that I could be reunited with the man for whom I had left everything behind. They took Alvarado and Santa Inez. We reached his place in about half an hour. Outside, in the middle of a group of men, I spotted my husband. I started to laugh and cry at the same time. It seemed impossible to me that we were finally going to be together. At the time, I thought that it would be forever. The car stopped in the middle of the street. I got out of the car and ran to meet him, just like in the movies. Crying, I embraced him. I couldn't stop staring at him. It seemed as though he might disappear. He put his arm around my waist. He paid the coyote. I said good-bye to La Nana. She gave me her telephone number just in case I needed it.

I couldn't sleep at all that night. I looked at him, and I couldn't believe that we were together again. I ran my fingers through his hair. I kissed the dimple in his chin. I buried my face into his chest. My love! My love! We were together. And now nothing could come between us.

He had already left by the time I woke up. The memory of my son stabbed me like a knife on our first day together. I comforted myself with the thought that La Nana could bring him across. "We cross children with papers," she had told me.

I started to straighten up his things. I had time to clean and tidy everything. When I was fixing up the things in his closet, I discovered a shoebox full of photographs. In one of them, Efraín was sitting in a park surrounded by roses, and a woman was stroking his chin. The same woman appeared again, waving from a car window. In another one, she was rubbing oil onto his back while the two lay on the beach. That moment turned into a lifetime of pain for me. "Help me, God."

The telephone rang urgently. I picked up the receiver. A woman's voice was looking for him and was surprised to hear my voice. She insisted on speaking with him. I told her that I was his wife. A painful silence could be heard on the other end of the line. She told me that she had been his girlfriend for six months now. Their wedding plans were well into the advanced stages. She told me her name. I gave her mine. I told her about Cristian and about our wedding in Ecuador. She kept quiet as if she was evaluating each of my words. She finally hung up without saying good-bye.

I dialed La Nana's number. I didn't want to see him again. I was liable to forget his betrayal and throw my arms around his neck. I thought he was more handsome now than ever, even though he had put on a few pounds and his hair was longer than before. I should have hated him, but I still loved him. I caught a plane to Ecuador that same night.

After a year, I decided to return to the United States. I met a wonderful man from Guatemala. We have been married for ten years now, and it has been the best thing that has ever happened to me.

Magdalena
Los Angeles, California

For the Love of My "Princess"

For a long time, my aunt had been telling me, "Why don't you go to the United States? You could work and go to school there. Your sister has already been there for a while now; and, together with your cousin, they could really help you get ahead."

I never wanted to leave Mexico. I had a degree in addition to experience working at a bank. I had always worked and worked so that I wouldn't succumb to the same fate as many of my compatriots; but, in the end, I was left with no other option.

One fine day, I was let go from my job. I tried to look for other employment but I realized that it wouldn't be easy to find another job. Nevertheless, I refused to get discouraged. The days began to go by, then months without being able to find a decent job. I was overworked and underpaid. I remember that the last job I was offered would pay 1,200 pesos a month. One could live on that kind of salary, but with a number of limitations. It wasn't enough to cover the cost of food, clothing, transportation, and education. I had no other choice than to say farewell to my "princess," promising her that I would write. I loved her very much. She swore that she would wait for me.

With the documents from my work at the bank, I was able to obtain a visa to the United States. I flew to Los Angeles by plane, with a very heavy heart but excited about the possibility of finding a good job for myself. I had a great deal of experience and education. My sister opened the doors of her house to me, but I felt out of place. I went out to look for work on a daily basis. Two months after my arrival, I found a job. I no longer had to worry about my papers because, thanks to the McArthur Park office of immigration, I had become a legal resident.

I filled out employment applications at different places each day. The first time that they called me in for an interview, I wore my finest suit. I shined my shoes with particular meticulousness; I put on my best tie; and my hair was impeccable. They gave me the job. It couldn't have been any other way: I was the most presentable and the one with the superior education. Unfortunately, the job that they offered me was to be a box-boy. One didn't need any special training to do that sort of work, just brute strength. I took the job out of pure necessity. My work consisted of carrying boxes of old files from the seventh to the fifteenth floor. I lasted six months, but nostalgia for my princess, my friends, and my city began to take its toll on me. Confident that my visa was in order, I decided to take a trip to Mexico for a few weeks, never imagining the turn that my life would take as a result of my journey.

My girlfriend started to cry as soon as she saw me: she had missed me very much. I had missed her very much, too. What I didn't expect was that she would want to go back with me to the United States. I told her that it would be impossible. She didn't have a passport, and I didn't have a job. I explained to her that the United States wasn't what they made it look like on TV, where everything is joy and plenty. It's a place full of stress and hard work. Things weren't so easy. My girlfriend wouldn't listen to me. The following afternoon, she showed up at my house with all of her stuff. I gave her a hug, excited by her spirit, but also worried about the uncertainty of our destiny. From that afternoon forward, my princess never went back home again.

I called someone I knew in Ciudad Juárez so that he could tell me what the border-crossing situation was like. "I have no idea," was his reply.

Meanwhile, my girlfriend's family was looking for me everywhere: they knew that she was with me. My physical well-being was in danger. We tried to hide, but they found us in the end; and after a few tears, reproaches, and reconciliation, we agreed to legalize our union with a justice of the peace, effective immediately. After the ceremony, they made plans to throw a reception. After the party, my savings were totally depleted.

The day after the legalization of our union, we flew to Ciudad Juárez. The only person I knew there was waiting for us. He didn't offer to let us stay at his house, but he did take us to one of the cheapest hotels. We stayed there. Our dinner on our first night as newlyweds consisted of two pieces of bread and a soda.

We had spent three days waiting in the hotel, and we had only eaten one hot meal. The "romerito" shrimp cakes that my sister wanted me to bring back for her ended up in our stomachs instead. Most of our money went to paying for the hotel, and we were left with precisely the amount we needed to return to Mexico City.

We had just decided to go back when someone came knocking on our door. It was a young lady, accompanied by three younger girls. They told us that my friend had told them about our situation and that they wanted to help.

"Get changed and make yourself pretty," the lady told my wife. "We're going to take you across by car."

We didn't know these people, but we decided to trust them. The border crossing would take place very early in the morning.

They came for her right on time. The hours went by; by midmorning, I began to wonder if I had done the right thing to trust them with my princess. When I noticed that morning had turned into afternoon, many thoughts began to race through my mind: *What if they're some sort of prostitution ring? What will I tell my mother-in-law when she asks? What if I never see her again?* I started to pace around the room. I would stop, from time to time, to look out the window. I would be frozen there, staring out the window. From there I could see the street. I don't know how many hours went by; all I know is that three figures suddenly appeared on the street, and one of them was my princess. I began to jump up and down like a madman. I felt so relieved.

"She couldn't get across, because they asked her a few questions and she didn't know how to respond," they explained. "Go change again. But, this time, put on some jeans," were the new instructions. She did what she was told, and I was left behind to wait once more, but this time a little less worried. The time went by slowly. The questions began to plague me once again: *Did they stop her? Did she make it to the other side?*

I lay down on the bed, staring at the ceiling and thinking about what I was going to do if she didn't show up before nightfall. Another knock on the door startled me. The lady's husband, a very short man, came to notify me: "Your wife is now on the other side. She's in El Paso."

I wanted to jump for joy. I wanted to hug him. Now it was my turn. The instructions were to take only one suitcase. I grabbed the first one that I saw. The other two were left behind. On my way out, I realized I had a problem: I didn't have any money to pay the bill. Sorrowfully, I took the gold chain that my princess had given to me on our wedding day and handed it over to the guy in charge.

The man took me with his wife, who was already waiting for us in the car. It turned out that her name was Julissa. "Your wife is fine. You should walk across with your visa to avoid any suspicions. We'll be waiting for you on the other side." I nodded my head.

Each step felt like walking a mile. My nervousness betrayed me. I regained my composure inches from standing before the Border Patrol officer. When he saw my suitcase, he asked what was inside. There were a few seconds of pause. At that moment I realized that I didn't know what was inside the bag.

"Open up the suitcase," he ordered. The lock sprang open and some shoes, a blow-dryer, makeup, and underwear could be seen. Intrigued, the immigration officer asked, "What is all this?"

"It's just stuff that I'm taking to my sister," I said without hesitation.

"Go ahead," the officer said dryly.

My heart began to slow down when we reached Julissa and her husband's house. Things couldn't have been better. The couple opened the doors of their house to us. Without any vested interest whatsoever, they helped us. Their five children, three young girls and two little ones, offered us their friendship. It was an experience that left us with many fond memories.

We completed the second phase of our journey by plane. We had $40. Thanks to our friends, we were able to put together enough money to pay for our fare to Los Angeles. My princess wore a tailored suit and makeup and did up her hair; I had on dress slacks and a gabardine shirt and carried a black work portfolio under my arm. As we passed through the metal detectors, two police officers focused their attention on me. I had to go back through again: "Beep." The policemen approached, and I moved to the side. They subjected me to the most scrutinizing search. The handheld detector showed nothing. So they let me go.

My wife had gone ahead and was waiting for me on the plane. Once seated, we intertwined our hands, sweaty with fear. I looked out the tiny window and watched the smooth take-off. I needed a drink. The voice of the captain announced a stop in Phoenix. I began to perspire again, now more intensely than before. "It's a direct flight. We're not supposed to go through Phoenix," I protested.

Nobody listened to me. The flight time was very short. We touched down at the Phoenix airport, and they informed us that we would have to board another airplane in order to continue on to Los Angeles. Two Border Patrol officers were watching us. I pretended to be concentrating on the papers that I had in my hand. My wife, with red hair and dark glasses, looked for something that she couldn't find in her purse. We passed by the two officers without stopping and took our seats on the plane. Los Angeles was getting closer.

The city lights were our sign that we were just about to land. A waiting room, a passageway, and a few flights of stairs were all that separated us from the door that opened onto the street. We didn't even want to claim our bags. First, I made sure to take my princess out to the sidewalk; she would be safe once outside. I returned for our suitcase. I was only a few feet away from the street when a shout sent icy chills through my veins. I thought they were after me, but it was somebody who wanted the claim ticket for my bag. I gave it to him and walked out to the street. We took a taxi directly to the apartment that I had left before my trip. My hand was shaking so much that I couldn't get the key to go into the lock. We laughed for a few minutes. Once inside, I wanted to scream and jump for joy. I had built up a lot of stress and anxiety.

Later, my princess told me that her experience crossing

the border had been terrifying. Without getting all of the precise details, I know that she swam through pestilent, rat-infested waters, she ran, and she jumped over fences in order to get across. I've decided not to ask her so that she won't have to remember it all again.

In fewer than three years, my princess and I have received our high school diplomas, and God and we both know that, with a little perseverance and the right preparation, we will go very far.

James
Gardena, California

She Had Just Given Birth

I had just turned nineteen, and the economic recovery that President Luis Echeverría Álvarez had promised had turned out to be nothing more than that—a promise. And like millions of other Mexicans, I had lost any desire to believe in him, and I had lost all hope that things in Mexico were going to improve. History would show that I made the right decision.

My neighborhood, Colonia Unidad Independencia, was like many other residential areas in Mexico City: full of dearth and privation, but there was a real sense of community. There was no loneliness, remorse, or even hunger. There was always enough money to get a bowl of *pozole* or eat some tacos for dinner at Doña Conchita's stand on the corner. And it was common for us to go out each afternoon and sit in the doorways and socialize with our neighbors from across the way.

But there were two reasons why I wanted to leave Mexico: my lack of confidence in the new president's ability to fulfill his promises, and the promise of adventure in traveling to the United States. I left Mexico on November 28, 1973.

I invested my life's savings in a bus ticket from Transportes Norte de Sonora. It cost me 350 pesos. I had 50 left for the remainder of my trip. I'm not sure how many days transpired, maybe two, maybe three, before I reached Tijuana. All I know is that we arrived on a very gloomy day. The watch on the guy sitting next to me showed eight o'clock in the evening.

With no money for a room, I went into a pool hall, and I slept there all night long. I was getting ready to leave the billiards room and go in search of a coyote, when someone told me that they could provide me with that service right there. One allowed me to join him. He understood my situation. We departed that very morning. Before getting into his car, I asked him if he could wait for me for a second. I ran into a liquor store and bought a bottle of tequila, then hid the little bit of money that was left over. I bought the booze in order to offset the effects of the cold, never dreaming that that bottle would help save a woman's life.

The coyote directed me to an abandoned house near Colonia Libertad. There were ten people waiting for him there: eight men and two women. I think my youthful appearance gave the two women confidence in me. They came up to me and began to strike up a conversation. They were mother and daughter. The daughter was fourteen years old, but I couldn't calculate her mother's age; she wasn't young, but she wasn't old, either. She told me that she and her daughter were coming from Zacatecas and that she had just given birth two days before to a son whom she had left in Zacatecas.

We were scheduled to depart that evening. We crossed through the airport. We walked by a few stables, and it was there that the coyote gave us the order to run. We all started running. We had gone about three miles when I realized that the two women had been left far behind. I went back for them. I noticed that the one who had just given birth was struggling to walk. We had to leap over cracks and traverse ravines, but she wasn't able to.

"Little by little, I've been losing my strength," she

explained.

Her daughter looked at her with a great deal of concern. She came up to me, and with tears in her eyes, she said, "Please help my mother. She can't take another step."

It was obvious that the women couldn't go on any longer. The coyote, along with the others, moved farther and farther away. I told the woman to hold on to me. We continued to walk when suddenly she fainted.

"Just leave me here. I can't go on any farther," she told us when she came to.

I brought out the bottle of tequila, and I rubbed some onto her face. She regained her composure and was able to keep walking. Along the way, she said, "Please don't leave us out here. It's very dangerous."

The coyote and the other people were now long gone. With them nowhere in sight, we continued to walk all night.

It was daybreak when we reached Encinitas, California. I was practically carrying the lady when she fainted again. I didn't even know her name. When I noticed that she had passed out, I quickly pulled out the tequila bottle and rubbed it on her once again. I used the whole bottle on her. She responded and recuperated to some degree.

I don't know where she gathered the strength, but she continued to walk until we reached the highway. We spotted a store and stopped there to rest. We bought hotdogs and soft drinks. There, we found some other people who helped us get to Los Angeles. I said goodbye to the two women without ever knowing their names.

Miguel Ángel
Los Angeles, California

Dreamers Never Lose Heart

We were living in the greatest country in the world, and it was a mistake to have left Honduras, where I was leading a life without want or privation. I was an insurance salesman by trade. I worked for the best company in the nation. I earned an average of 50,000 lempiras. I was also enrolled in my fourth year of law school at the National Autonomous University of Honduras.

My wife was an administrative assistant for the controller at the same insurance company. Between the two of us, we made a very comfortable living. We lived well. We took two vacations each year. We had a housekeeper. The elder of our two children attended private school, and our nucleus of friends were all upper middle class.

A friend living in the United States started to call me on a daily basis, encouraging me to join him. He filled my head with promises that would later prove to be false. We traveled to the United States by plane without any complications. The problem was that, though we searched and searched for the friend who had made so many promises, the one who called every day, we never found him.

We came to suffer a great deal in this country. It has been a daily struggle. It's not easy to earn a living that allows us to support our children, but we never lose heart.

A dream, perhaps the most important factor inspiring me to continue the struggle, is not to allow this country to defeat me. I am a dreamer, and dreamers never give up.

My advice for all of those who are already here is: fight to get ahead, and please, do not convince anyone else to come and suffer in this country. We wouldn't want our families and friends to suffer as we have suffered.

What keeps my wife and me going here are two very strong motivators: the love that we share as a couple and the love that we have for our children.

Fernando
Los Angeles, California

They're Coming after Us

I couldn't go on, but Juan, my stepfather, grabbed me by the hand and said, "Keep running. We're almost there." We continued to run, but we were forced to stop because many of the older ladies who came with us couldn't take another step. I was the youngest girl in the group.

We hid behind a groove of trees. Around five minutes later, we had to run, run, and run again until we reached the second hiding place. Once there, they hid us in some trash-cans. A few minutes passed, and they took us out so we could slip through a wire mesh fence. We were now in San Isidro, California. We thought we were safe: we had already made it to the other side. We caught our breath. We massaged our tired limbs. Then we continued our walk until we reached the freeway. Night had fallen upon us. Cold, wet, and hungry, we huddled up together to pass the night under the freeway. We hadn't gotten any sleep when morning broke into a new day.

Our new orders were to board a van as soon as it arrived. We didn't have to wait long. The van was very punctual, and it didn't stop until we reached Oceanside. We were forced to wait there until they closed the Border Patrol checkpoint. Two hours of waiting went by, and we switched into another van. We were passing through the immigration checkpoint when the coyote told us, "They're coming after us. I'm going to pull over. Everyone jump out and start running. You don't know who's driving."

We became very nervous. The coyote briefly increased his speed so he could pull over suddenly to the side of the road. We all made a mad dash, but the Border Patrol surrounded us and rounded everybody up. We were all wet and handcuffed on the shoulder of the freeway. At that moment, my dreams of ever trying to cross again disappeared. They deported us to Tijuana.

That very same day, we decided to give it another try with a different coyote. Without even waiting for night to fall, the new coyote explained to us that he would cross us in a van in which they had removed the seats. The hole only fit one person. I was the one to go first. Balled up in that tiny space and covered up with a carpet and a tire on top of my head, I could hear the Border Patrol agent's footsteps. He asked the coyote, in Spanish, for his papers. I could also hear the growling of the dogs that were sniffing around the tire. I knew I had been caught; I was just waiting for someone to say, "All right, get out of there." But, instead, I heard the van start to pull away. I thought I was going to faint with relief. A small door opened later. "You can get out of there until we get to the second checkpoint."

Before reaching the second immigration checkpoint, I got into a different car with somebody else. We passed through without any problem, and we pulled off at one of the cities in order to wait for Juan. We were very happy to have made it, safe and sound.

Sheila
Los Angeles, California

Mine Is the Same Story as So Many Other Children

Mexicali is a city that shares the border with Calexico, California. Few places in the world are as hot as Mexicali. Many people go there hoping to cross to the other side, not knowing that it's much more difficult to enter the United States by passing through Mexicali. The border crossing in Mexicali is small. There aren't as many bridges going across as there are in Tijuana. The Border Patrol officers have more time to inspect one's documents because there are fewer people crossing, but the people coming from southern Mexico and Central America aren't aware of that.

Those who come to cross the border gather in Parque Chapultepec close to the line. There, they sleep, eat, bathe, and some even hang their clothes from the treetops. The women find shade under the trees. Children look disfigured staring at the sun in anguish.

I remember how the fence dividing Calexico from Mexicali got thicker and thicker as the years went by. One day, the chainlink fence full of holes disappeared, and a solid metal wall topped with barbed wire appeared in its place. It was if they had built it over night. Additional Border Patrol officers also appeared to keep watch over the border. The newspapers spoke of a militarization of the border, but I never saw any soldiers, just immigration officers.

My job was to help the ladies who crossed the border to buy their bread, milk, and eggs in Calexico. I situated myself at the exit to the border crossing and offered my services to assist them. Relieved, they would unload their heavy bags onto me, and I would accompany them to the bus stop in exchange for spare change. That was my job. Some of them already knew me, and my services were widely sought after. I became part of the border landscape. The same immigration officials would watch me, and they wouldn't even get upset when a tiny act of carelessness caused me to cross to the other side in order to find a woman carrying her grocery bags. For me, it was natural to cross into Calexico without any papers, until the idea of going beyond the border crossing presented itself.

My father was sold on the idea, and the attempt nearly cost us our lives. We were going to cross through the desert around Yuma, Arizona. There were seven people, my dad and me among them. The first step was to cross the river. A person who could swim very well was in charge of taking us across one by one. Climbing on top of an inner tube, the swimmer took us to the other side of the river. We all made it just fine.

The problems began in the desert. The hike became very difficult once the temperature reached one hundred degrees Fahrenheit. The sun made everything harder on us. We prayed for the night to fall, but the setting of the sun didn't make things any easier. Taking advantage of the night, we walked for many hours. The sun rose and set again. It seemed as though three days had gone by, and we continued to walk.

We had no more food or water. One of the men in the group collapsed onto a rock. "You guys go on. I can't do it anymore."

The leader of the group told us: "Let's go. He can stay if he wants to. We'll just leave him behind."

My dad, who also looked very tired, said defiantly, "You know what? Screw you! Either we all get out of this alive, or we can all go to hell together."

I was surprised to hear him so determined. Our guide tried to argue, but my dad would not back down. "Go on ahead. But we're going to stay with this man here and see what God has to say about all of this."

The coyote went along with the rest, and we stayed with the man. We stared at each other not knowing what to do or where to go. The fallen man stared at us too. We stayed like that for a long time. Suddenly, the guide appeared. He had come back because he discovered that he was lost.

It was nighttime. A large, circular moon, as white as a piece of jack cheese, illuminated our faces. The moon was absolutely beautiful. My dad stood up and said, "The moon will be our guide."

Everybody got up and began to walk. I don't know how much time had gone by, but the sun had started to rise when we spotted a well. We leaned over and on the bottom we saw a puddle of water full of bugs and insects. The water looked very dirty. Luckily, we had not thrown away all of the empty water jugs that we were carrying. Since I was the smallest, I had to jump in with the jugs and fill them up. I went down until I reached that smelly pond. There was a cave, and as I got closer, I could see an image of the Virgin of Guadalupe. I filled the water jugs. I put a piece of my shirt over one of them like a strainer and took a drink. As thirsty as I was, it tasted like spring water. Once I was back up on the ground, and after everyone had quenched their thirst, we resumed our march. Fatigue was falling upon us once again, when an enormous river full of crystal-clear water appeared before us. We bathed there and rested for a short while. We did the last stretch of the way without stopping, until we had reached a ranch where they gave jobs to my dad and some of the others. They didn't want to employ me because I was under age. I wasn't discouraged, and I left to go pick cherries. I ended up eating more than I picked.

Months went by, and my routine was to work and to save money. My birthday came, and from very early that morning, I knew that something special was going to happen to me. And so it was: the Border Patrol arrested me and deported me to Mexicali. But I refused to quit. A short time later, I crossed back over again following the same route, and I promised myself that I would never get caught again. Many months of working and saving passed by.

I hadn't gone back to my homeland in ten years. Nostalgia took its toll on me, particularly on the nights when I would recall the afternoons when we would eat *raspado* ices and *carne asada* tacos. Thanks to the new amnesty bill, I was able to get my papers in order, and I will soon become a citizen. Now I'll be able to come and go as I please.

I dedicate this story to the children of border towns who go out into the streets in search of spare change so that they can buy their parents and siblings something to eat.

Antonio
Panorama City, California

A Pack of Tortillas Was All We Had to Eat

It was nighttime when we crossed the line under a fine, gentle rain, the kind that seeps into everything. We walked completely out in the open. We wore plain clothing. We didn't posses any form of protection. My wife and our six-year-old son traveled with me. A friend of mine would take my two younger boys across the line.

All three of us crossed into San Isidro, California, without any problems. Once there, they put us in the trunk of a car destined for the blessed City of Angels. It was March 16, 1979. I marked that day as if it were my second date of birth. The first one, coincidentally, was March 16, 1949.

Like any good dreamer, I only thought that I would live in the United States for around three years, save about $3,000 and then return to Mexico. We made it to Los Angeles owing $500. For the first couple of weeks, we survived on a single pack of tortillas per day. Those were the most difficult two weeks of our life as a family. That was March 1979. By June of that same year, we had already paid the $500 we owed for our crossing; and, one year later, our first daughter was born in this country.

I think that, like so many others, my plans also changed. The initial idea was to save money and to allow my family to see how people lived in the United States. By October 1981, we had saved $4,500, with which we decided to buy a house. My children had already begun to speak English. We postponed our return to Mexico for another year. All of this waiting resulted in three more children. We wanted to make it an even half-dozen. That's how the years came and went—"next year we'll go"—we stayed for twenty years.

Thanks to my wife's wise use of money, we were able to pay off the house that cost us $65,000 in seven years. I remember how, after having sent our last house payment, we decided to buy new clothes for our children for the very first time. The lady at the store where we bought clothes for our kids told us that things were getting harder and harder in the United States.

I would tell anyone who is coming here that things are difficult but not impossible. It's all about hard work and perseverance. If someone were to ask me how we did it, I would quote this phrase to them: "The basis of economic prosperity is hard work and spending wisely."

Just as we have succeeded, others can succeed as well. Immigrants don't come here looking for handouts; we are contributing a great deal to the prosperity of this country.

Heriberto
Los Angeles, California

Could It Be the Feathers in Our Hats?

Right now it seems like I've turned the right key in the lock of my memory, because all of my recollections are coming to mind. I left Zacatecas very much against my own will, because I had worked very hard to get ahead with my family. I owned a van in Mexico. I sold it and bought an American minivan. Without asking permission from anyone, much less the government, I established my own taxi service as if the vehicle were a passenger van.

The authorities would hassle me often. They wouldn't allow me to work. They demanded that I buy a domestic model. So that's what I did: I sold the minivan, and I established another small shuttle service. But the problems continued because my van was illegal. I asked my father-in-law for the money to buy a van with national plates. Four years went by, and the engine and the tires both gave out, and everything on the van was falling apart, too. I was left with no money and no van. Once again, my father-in-law loaned me money to buy another one in the Unites States. And that's when my adventure began.

I went to Tijuana thinking that crossing the border was going to be easy. I contacted a guide. I won't call them "coyotes" because I know now that they're really wolves. They easily sniff out those of us who want to cross to the other side, and they come up to us. Is it something in our voices?

The feathers in our hats? Our serapes? They walk up to you and they begin to brainwash you: "Hey, man, we're going to go for it tonight. All you need is enough money for the fare and the taxis." Very innocently, you fall. "Do you have twenty pesos that you can loan me? I'll pay you back later." And weakly, naively, with the hope of getting across, you loan him the money just to be deceived time and again. You just can't tell which way the current is flowing, and all of the brainwashing doesn't end, until someone really takes you to that line of sheet-metal fencing.

We caught up with them sitting, watching the other side, counting the immigration vehicles that, because of their formation and green color, looked like vines clinging to the hillside. I sat down, too, and so we were all staring at the other side. The clock struck one o'clock in the morning, then two, and then three. The guide told us, "Grab a piece of cardboard and go to sleep, because it's not going to happen tonight. Today's not the day." I lay down, and after a short while, I started to feel an itch all over my body. Another guy told me, "It's the fleas. There's a lot of them around here."

That same night, I went back to sleep in the same room where I had been staying. But before I fell asleep, I remembered what the guide had said, "Today's not the day." I began to question how he knew that it wasn't the day.

On the following morning, I took a bath, and I put on the same clothes as the day before. I didn't have any others. I ate a big breakfast and went back to the spot where the group was staying. A whole day went by. Night fell and the sun rose again, and we were still there, staring at the Border Patrol. I took a recount of the money that I still had remaining: $90 and $500 pesos. I decided to go buy some things at the flea market. I left with two pairs of cheap pants, three shirts, and five pairs of socks. I put everything on at the same time. It was difficult for me to walk with so many clothes on.

It was the same old routine, and the guide told us again, "Today's not the day."

I began to get frustrated. I prayed to my patron saints that the waiting would soon be over. The next day, I didn't want to wait anymore. So I decided to look for another guide to cross through Tecate. I immediately contracted someone to take me across. We bought water and other utensils; but as we were leaving the store, we were stopped by Mexican immigration officers. They were looking for a few guides who had abandoned some people. They kept us in jail for a day then they cut us loose. After that, my money started to run pretty low so I was only eating one meal a day. Three days later, I tried to cross through Tecate again. All we did was sit around and wait. So I decided to try making it through the border. That was a big mistake: they arrested me; and after rigorous interrogation and almost a whole day of waiting, they gave us a frozen hamburger, some apple juice, and an orange. At that moment, I realized that I had not eaten all day long, and I thanked God for the food.

They deported us at around seven in the morning on the following day. I was hungry. I decided to spend my last few pesos on a big breakfast: four tamales and a *champurrado*. I couldn't sleep that night. I decided to go back to the original group. There, I found them telling each other stories so that the time would go by faster. That day, the guide came to the same conclusion: "Today isn't the day, either. Go to sleep."

Nobody complained. "Well, what are they waiting for?" I thought to myself. I decided to try another guide. "I'm going to take you through Tecate."

"Tecate again?" I asked.

He assured me that this time it would be different. We reached Tecate, and we started to climb a very tall mountain. The Border Patrol spotted us, and we fell back in order to give it another try that evening. Night came, and we started to hike up the same mountain, all uphill. I was out of breath. I sat down on a rock to rest. We kept on walking. I was very thirsty, but we didn't bring any water. We didn't make it very far, because a Border Patrol vehicle was right there waiting for us. Some of the guys started to run, but I just stayed there, thirsty as hell. They found three other guys farther down the road. Once in the van, one of them, thanks be to God, offered me some water and a few rolled tacos. "Hey, man, you want some?" I drank a ton of water and ate three tacos. They transferred us to another van. Another round of rigorous interrogation, then they threw us out at three o'clock in the morning. We all rode in on a bus. I couldn't sleep. I was admiring the landscape along the way and praying. I thought that, because I was thirty-eight years old and weighed around two hundred thirty pounds, I was a pretty fat *pollo,* and that's why they kept catching me. With these and other thoughts, we reached the border early in the morning. I bought a coffee and sat down on a bench to admire the spectacle of Americans who entered our country, predominant young people. And it occurred to me at that very moment, "How come they can come into our country whenever they feel like it and do whatever they please?" That's when I began to think that there shouldn't be any borders.

I went to the first group. I spent a few more days resting and going to church to ask the saints for the day that the guide was waiting to come. I didn't exactly understand which day he was waiting for, but when it came, we all knew it. It was like a miracle: the sun began to rise, and a sort of mist covered up all of the searchlights like a giant sheet. Nothing could be seen. He told us, "Today's the day. Now we can go. Come on."

We hopped over the sheet metal fencing and marched nonstop across many roads. Since we were protected by the fog, there was no way for them to detect us. I don't know how many hours we walked, but it was a lot. We showed up very tired and completely soaked. I thanked God and our guide. I reached Los Angeles twenty-six pounds lighter and with only $30 pesos in my pocket.

Salvador
La Puente, California

Everyone from the North Shows up Looking "All Fly"

I decided to go to the United States, because everyone from up north who came back to visit León, Guanajuato, showed up looking "all fly." I was sixteen when I made up my mind to go to the United States, with or without my parents's permission. I wanted to have the same things that those people from up north had: cars, clothes, jewelry. I was never going to have that in Guanajuato, and I knew that there were a lot of jobs in the United States. I convinced two friends of mine to come with me; and without giving it much thought, we left for Tijuana to cross into the Unites States from there.

We contracted a coyote in Tijuana. He told us that he would charge us $300 to take us to Los Angeles. He gave us a time to meet him at the beach in Tijuana, and twelve other people showed up at the scheduled time. We waited until it was dark, and the instructions were to walk, run, duck down, and walk some more. After two hours, the coyote told us, "Get down on the ground. If the Border Patrol catches you, tell them that you were crossing on your own."

The Border Patrol passed by without stopping. We got to a little house, like a farmhouse. There were already about thirty people there. The coyotes started making little groups. They wanted to separate me from my friends, but we wouldn't let them. They put us in a group of ten. As soon as we were ready, they took us out on another hike. This one was much longer. We walked through puddles, mud bogs, trails, ravines, and shrubs. Falling, ducking, and pulling ourselves along the way, we reached the freeway.

A four-door sedan was waiting for us. There were two coyotes sitting in the front seat of the car. We were among the first to get in. They made all three of us squat down in the back of the car. They put a whole family—mom, dad, and four kids—in one seat. Five children fit inside the trunk. The car took off, burning rubber. It felt like we were going a thousand miles an hour. The kids on the floor were scared and crying. They were bumping into each other and bouncing on the ground like marbles. "Shut up!" yelled the coyote.

We went on like that all the way to the inspection station. I knew that it would take a miracle for them not to notice so many people in one car. And the miracle happened. At the exact moment when he should have looked our way, the Border Patrol officer turned his head to the other side to light a cigarette. He waved us by with his hand. We drove through, and there were no more stops or inspections. The coyotes took us to our own destinations.

Olga Lidia
Hollywood, California

They Told Me That You Could Make a Lot of Money

They told me that you could make a lot of money and live very well in the United States. And that's why we sold the few things that we had in order to have money for the trip. The worst thing was that we didn't have enough money to take the bus, much less a plane, so we ended up buying tickets for the train. The train moved very slowly. First, you heard this "chug-a-chug-a, chug-a-chug-a." It felt like we were standing still. The only way you could tell that we were moving was to look at the light-posts that were being left behind. And so, our days of travel continued slowly. I remember how the people felt suffocated inside of the rail-cars. There was no air-conditioning. We were all squished together. My wife looked at what I was carrying in my arms. She smiled, thinking about our only treasure.

We finally reached Mexicali, and from there we went to Tijuana: my wife, myself and our little bundle—it was all that we had. We stayed in Tijuana for three days as my brothers-in-law arranged for someone to take us across. They found a guy who tried to cross us through the foothills. He warned me that it was dangerous to take my bundle with me because the Border Patrol could take it away. I told him that they would have to kill me first. They also insisted that I leave it with them, promising that they would take it to me later. But my wife and I wouldn't give in.

Our first attempt was at night. I carried the bundle. And my wife wouldn't let it out of her sight. We hiked through the foothills, but they caught us the first time. We went back and tried again, and this time we ended up in jail. The Border Patrol agent noticed what I had been carrying in my arms. They set us free the following day. We tried it again with someone else. This time, we made it. The couple took us to the other side of the border.

The bundle that I carried in my arms is now ten years old. He's going to school, and whenever I can, I buy books for him to read. He has a little brother who is three, a year and a half older than he was when we marched through the foothills on that chilly night.

Benito
Los Angeles, California

We Landed in France, Not in New York

What are you gonna do, honey? Castro's guards showed up and demanded our house. That's exactly how it happened, back in 1972. What do you do when someone just shows up and gives you an hour to clear out of your own house? I'm telling you, honey, just like that. The guards from Cuban immigration came to the front door and told us that we had an hour to pack everything up. We had already made plans to leave the country two days later, but not at that very moment. Imagine how my poor grandmother felt! And my mom and dad, my brother, and my sister, too. I don't know if you know, but when a Cuban leaves his country, the only thing they let him take out of his house is a picture of his patron saint, and we took along our own Virgin of Santa Barbara.

Well, you can imagine how worn-out we were in those two days that we had to wait before we could leave. And, sweetheart, don't think for a second that anybody wanted us in their house; they were afraid of what Castro would do. They were all afraid until an aunt of my mom's took pity on us and let us stay with her. What a beautiful thing she did; an act of love like that doesn't happen much.

On the day we were supposed to leave, we had to go without any luggage because they didn't let us take anything out of the country, not a thing. We didn't even have money, because back then they threw anyone they found with a dollar on him into jail for "smuggling illegal currency."

We didn't bring any Cuban money because Cuban currency isn't worth a thing in the rest of the world; it's worth less than any other currency. So we left with nothing; we flew twenty-four hours; and then, get this, when we thought we were finally getting to New York, we landed in France! Honey, I have no idea how that happened.

They had us all get off the plane, and they took us to a waiting room in the airport. We were there for about two hours, and then we got back on the very same plane and headed to Spain. It was September 6, 1972. Once we got there, the Spanish authorities didn't know what to do with us. They weren't counting on that flight. They held us for a long time, and it was freezing cold. Can you believe it? Leaving the Cuban sun and heading straight into an icebox! With no money and no one to help us or tell us where to go, we sat down on the floor in a corner of the airport. No, honey, don't be foolish; they wouldn't even give us a glass of water. When I tried to ask a stewardess for a glass of water for my mother, who was dying of thirst, you know what she said? "I don't give water to any anti-communist." Those very words, that's exactly what she said.

We left the airport, and a taxicab driver, whom I call "our guardian angel," saw the state we were in and took us to a hostel; in Spain that's what they call hotels like Motel Six. Honey, when that angel of ours said good-bye that night, I swear I thought he would fly right up into the sky. We thought we would never see him again, but we were wrong. Can you believe it? He came back with his arms full of sweets and hot coffee. When my father saw that incredible kindness, he started to cry.

Before he left, our angel said, "There's always a better tomorrow. One day, you all will do the same for somebody else. Then, this debt you have with me today will be paid."

The next day, our spirits were up again. My mom asked the hostel owner for permission to call the United States so she could get my aunt to send some money. The woman wouldn't let her call, and she put a lock on the telephone. We needed to find a way to get some money sent to us. So we figured we'd have to head out to the streets to beg.

We didn't know where to go. Do you have any idea what the cold is like in Europe? It's so cold that it gets into your bones. Well, anyway, let me get back to the story. We kept walking, and we finally came to a Catholic church; we felt like the Virgin of Santa Barbara had opened up the doors to heaven for us. They would help us in there for sure. We stepped into the church, feeling certain we'd get some hot food. But when the priest saw us, he just said, "I'm sorry, my children; I can't help you."

We walked out of the church feeling completely disappointed.

Oh, honey, I can't tell you how we walked those streets with nowhere to go and nothing to look for until finally we ran into another one of our angels. He said that a lot of Cubans were regulars at the Galaxia café, just about a block away. We found the place, and a man named Félix helped us out. He put us up, fed us, and let us call my aunt. Another man, Lázaro, took us to a Masonic temple, where they gave us coats, clothes, and bags of food. We were relieved, but the cold and the malnutrition had already taken their toll on my mother's health; because just a little bit after that, she almost died on me.

Later on, we finally arrived in the United States, and I got a chance to think about everything we had suffered through to have a better life.

Pilar
Los Angeles, California